Caroline M. Noel

The NAME of JESUS

and other Poems

Caroline M. Noel

The NAME of JESUS
and other Poems

ISBN/EAN: 9783741123214

Manufactured in Europe, USA, Canada, Australia, Japa

Cover: Foto ©Lupo / pixelio.de

Manufactured and distributed by brebook publishing software (www.brebook.com)

Caroline M. Noel

The NAME of JESUS

THE NAME OF JESUS

AND OTHER POEMS,

For the Sick and Lonely.

BY

CAROLINE M. NOEL.

NEW EDITION. FOURTEENTH THOUSAND.

LONDON:
HATCHARDS, PICCADILLY.
1876.

To S. N.

When I give thanks to God, for all
  His priceless gifts to me,
Believe that then, among the chief,
  I give Him thanks for thee.

For all the love that He has rained
  Upon me, from thine eyes,
That shine like stars above my storms,
  Calm, though they sympathize.

And if one day the hands must loose,
  That now so fondly clasp,
Yet, e'en though parted, both will be
  Within the same strong grasp.

One on Christ's bosom gently laid,
  The other safely led
A longer road, unto the land
  Where live the blessèd Dead.

There meeting, who can guess the gleam
  Of rapture, that will rise,
When we the light of that fair realm
  See in each other's eyes?

O deep unspeakable repose
  Of knowing, that for aye
All that disturbed and hindered love
  Has wholly passed away!

Sin, sickness, sorrow, chills of age,
  And pangs of mortal fear,
Can never reach the land where Christ
  Has wiped away each tear.

For Death has no dominion there,
  Where Sin has never trod,
But souls transfigured, live and love,
  Within the Life of God.

    Then fear we not to trust His Word,
      And cherish Love's increase;
    Since e'en its sharpest throes must pass
      Into Eternal Peace.

Easter, 1868.

PREFACE TO THE THIRD EDITION.

THESE Verses were printed in their rough unfinished state, just as they were written down at the dictation of one, who is incapacitated by weakness for the task of revision and correction. As they have met with unusual acceptance from many of those for whom they were intended, they are again published, with considerable additions.

May He, Who was anointed that He might "comfort all that mourn," vouchsafe to give them some further employment in His Ministry of Consolation!

October, 1863.

CONTENTS.

	PAGE
THE NAME OF JESUS	1
INDWELLING	5
GOD OF ALL LOVE AND PITY	8
THE YOKE	10
WINCHESTER CATHEDRAL	14
SUBMISSION	17
PASSING HENCE	19
CHASTISEMENT	21
RETROSPECT	24
THE PILGRIM	27
STILL WATERS	29
A CONTRAST	32
SELF-ACCUSATION	35
DISAPPOINTMENT	37
"UPBRAIDETH NOT"	39
THE ANNUNCIATION	42
THE DIVINE INFANCY	45
"HE LAID HIS HAND UPON ME"	48
BETHANY	50
GOOD FRIDAY	54
WOMAN'S COMMISSION	57
DAY-BREAK	62

CONTENTS.

	PAGE
ASCENSION DAY	65
"THE LORD AND GIVER OF LIFE"	68
HIDE ME	72
THE LOVE OF GOD	75
THE CROSS	79
IN PAIN	81
HOLY COMMUNION	83
THE NET	86
ASSOCIATIONS	88
NIGHT	91
THE SEA SHORE	95
DYING	97
WAITING	98
PARADISE	100
THE REDEMPTION OF THE BODY	105
GATHERED FLOWERS	109
AFTER DARK	111
HOME	114
USELESSNESS	117
REST	120
OFFERINGS	122
WEARINESS	124
GOOD NIGHT	127
GONE BEFORE	129
DEATH	132
DESOLATION	135
SELF-DEDICATION	139
ON AN INFANT'S GRAVE	141
A LITTLE WHILE	142

CONTENTS.

	PAGE
THANKSGIVING	143
ALPHA	145
ALPHA AND OMEGA	147
MEMORIALS	151
TWILIGHT	156
ON THE DEATH OF A CHILD	158
TO * * *	160
HIS PRESENCE	163
THE PAST	166
H. L. P.	169
IN MEMORIAM,—	
SATISFIED	170
ASLEEP	171
SILENCE	172
HERE AND THERE	173
SUNSET AND SUNRISE	175
CROWNED	178
A FRAGMENT	180
MISSIONARY HYMN	181
"OUR LIGHT AFFLICTION"	183
WELCOMED	184
ALICE	187
"EVEN SO, LORD JESUS"	189

ORDER

FOR THE

VISITATION OF THE SICK.

The Almighty Lord, Who is a most strong Tower to all them that put their trust in Him, to Whom all things in Heaven, in Earth, and under the Earth, do bow and obey, be now and evermore thy defence; and make thee know and feel, that there is none other Name under Heaven given to Man, in whom, and through whom, thou mayest receive health and Salvation, but only the name of our Lord Jesus Christ. Amen.

THE NAME OF JESUS,

AND

OTHER POEMS.

The Name of Jesus.

ONE Name alone in all this death-struck earth,
One Name alone come down from highest heaven,
Whence healing and salvation we receive,
    To sinful man is given.

Name brought by Gabriel from the heart of God,
And laid like flower-seed in the adoring breast
Of her, in whom the mystery was wrought,
    And God made manifest:

O Name of Jesus!—of that lowly Babe
That on the sunny slopes of Nazareth strayed,
Or, calm and silent on the cottage floor,
    With wild flowers played:

B

Name of the wondrous Child, that in the temple stood,
With brow all meekness, and with eye all light,
Who to the blinded teachers of the Law
        Would have given sight:

Name of the Prophet, Healer, Master, Friend,
Death's mighty Vanquisher, and sorrow's Cure,
The Fountain of new innocence for man,
        That ever shall endure:

The secret, the unutterable Name,
From the world's earlier ages hid so long,
Now in time's fulness given at length to be
        The new creation's song:

And yet it was the scorn of Jewish lips,
And written by unholy heathen pen,
Then nailed aloft upon the awful Cross,
        Signal to God and men;

But never written in the dust of death,
Nor cut upon the portals of the grave,
So quickly He that threshold has recrossed,
        Triumphantly to save.

It dropped from Heaven like gently falling plume,
Just when the shadow of the white cloud fell
Upon the Apostles' upward-turnèd brows:
    "O wherefore dwell,

Ye Galilæans, gazing up so long
Into the clear blue depths ye search in vain?
Lo! this same Jesus, rising to His Throne,
    Shall so return again."

Once more Heaven sent it down upon the earth,
When from Love's central Fount the accents came,
And on the persecuting Saul poured down,
    In glory and in flame.

O Name of value infinite! and yet
Thou mov'st our spirits with a deeper thrill,
For the dear lips that have Thy music breathed,
    And then grown still.

For Thou the last gift art our lost ones leave,
To be our comfort on our onward way;
"Love Jesus," "Jesus is our only hope,"
    Adoringly they say.

As shipwrecked sailors grasp an oar, and launch
Upon the billows of a midnight sea,
These fearless souls, embracing "Jesus," plunge
    Into Eternity:

Then, safely floated to the Home of peace,
Where the bright plumèd angels throng the shore,
Still, still the Name of Jesus those glad hosts
    In anthems pour.

Name that the ransomed souls for ever wear,
Gemmed with pure lustre on each perfect brow,
Be Thou the radiance of our earthly lives;
    Transform us even now.

O Name above all names the most beloved!
Fullest of memories, and of untold peace,
Earnest of all unutterable joys!—
    Yet, fond heart, cease,

For Jesus is the Name of the High God:
Hushed be thy thoughts, and silently adore!
When thou shalt come to see Him as He is,
    Thou shalt know more.

Indwelling.

DRAW nigh unto my soul,
    O Holiest, draw nigh;
For I have wants within, which Thou
    Alone canst satisfy:
O deign to commune with me as I kneel;
Thy glory in my inmost soul reveal.

Thou speakest in Thy works;
    But, wondrous though they be,
They have no voice to utter forth,
    "Jesus has died for me:"
They show Thy goodness and Thy power divine,
But oh! they cannot tell me Thou art mine.

Nor is it, Lord, enough
    To see Thine image glow,
Reflected in Thy chosen ones
    Militant here below:
Thyself alone can satisfy the heart,
Thou art the only friend death cannot part.

Pleasant it is to stand
  Within Thy temples fair,
To hear Thy Ministers proclaim,
  That Thou dost meet us there; —
To kneel before Thine Altar and partake
The sacramental food for Jesu's sake.

But pain and death will come;
  And then, O God, for me
Can Anthem, Litany, and Prayer
  In aught availing be?
The melodies that float through choir and aisle,
While cold in dust my head shall rest the while?

Draw near and condescend
  To take up Thine abode
Within this sinful heart, and dwell,
  An ever-present God.
Must I not be alone with Thee at last?
Oh let my life be in Thy presence passed.

Father, my soul would be
  Like a transparent haze,
Through which Thy Deity should pour
  Its sanctifying rays.

Lord, fill me with Thy fulness; give me grace
To commune with Jehovah face to face.

 Reveal Thyself e'en now
  Within that inmost bound,
 Where the Immortal Essence dwells
  In solitude profound;
Where thought is lost, and strong emotions keep
Their ceaseless watch above the mystery deep.

 Do with me what Thou wilt,
  Low at Thy feet I fall;
 Absorb me in Thyself; be Thou,
  Father, my all in all:
Show me the glorious beauty that is Thine,
And the deep lowliness that should be mine.

God of all Love and Pity.

GOD of all love and pity,
   Thy children gently guide;
With heavenly food supply us,
   All needful good provide.

By waters still, refresh us,
   As patiently we wait,
Till Thou, the Fount of brightness,
   Our souls illuminate.

Our wishes and affections,
   Our impulses and powers,
We yield unto Thy guidance;
   For they are Thine, not ours.

Our spirits we surrender,
   Our purposes resign,
To be conformed for ever
   Unto the Will Divine.

With strong attraction draw us
  Unto Thyself alone,
O King of Saints, and bring us
  Unto Thy sapphire throne.

And till the morning dawneth
  For each tired soul's release,
Sustain us with the brightness
  Of Thine own perfect peace.

The Yoke.

SAVIOUR! beneath Thy yoke
    My wayward heart doth pine,
All unaccustomed to the stroke
    Of love divine:
Thy chastisements, my God, are hard to bear,
Thy cross is heavy for frail flesh to wear.

    "Perishing child of clay!
        Thy sighing I have heard;
    Long have I marked thy evil way,
        How thou hast erred:
Yet fear not; by My own most Holy Name,
I will shed healing through thy sin-sick frame."

    Praise to Thee, gracious Lord!
        I fain would be at rest;
    O now fulfil Thy faithful word,
        And make me blest!
My soul would lay her heavy burden down,
And take with joyfulness the promised crown.

"Stay, thou short-sighted child:
 There is much first to do;
Thy heart, so long by sin defiled,
 I must renew:
Thy will must here be taught to bend to Mine,
Or the sweet peace of heaven can ne'er be thine."

Yea, Lord, but Thou canst soon
 Perfect Thy work in me,
Till, like the pure calm summer moon,
 I shine by Thee;
A moment shine, that all Thy power may trace,
Then pass in silence to my heavenly place.

"Ah, coward soul! confess
 Thou shrinkest from My cure,
Thou tremblest at the sharp distress
 Thou must endure;
The foes on every hand for war arrayed,
The thorny path in tribulation laid.

"The process slow of years,
 The discipline of life,—
Of outward woes and secret tears,
 Sickness and strife,—

The idols taken from thee one by one,
Till thou canst dare to live with Me alone.

"Some gentle souls there are,
   Who yield unto My love,
Whom, ripening fast beneath My care,
   I soon remove;
But thou stiff-neckèd art, and hard to rule,
Thou must stay longer in affliction's school."

My Maker and my King!
   Is this Thy love to me?
O that I had the lightning's wing
   From earth to flee!
How can I bear the heavy weight of woes
Thine indignation on Thy creature throws?

"Thou canst not, O My child;
   So hear My voice again:
I will bear all thy anguish wild,
   Thy grief—thy pain;
My arms shall be around thee day by day,
My smile shall cheer thee on thy heavenward way.

"In sickness I will be
  Watching beside thy bed,
In sorrow thou shalt lean on Me
  Thy aching head.
In every struggle thou shalt conqueror prove,
Nor death itself shall sever from My love."

O grace beyond compare!
  O love most high and pure!
Saviour, begin, no longer spare!
  I can endure:
Only vouchsafe Thy grace, that I may live
Unto Thy glory, Who canst so forgive.

Winchester Cathedral.

WE stood beside the sculptured screen,
    And heard the holy sound
Of music, from the choir within,
    Filling the silence round.

We heard it rise and float and fall,
    Yet could not catch the words,
Which, to the worshippers within,
    Blent with those solemn chords.

But as each Psalm drew near its close,
    We knew that they would raise,
Unto the Lord Omnipotent,
    Ascriptions of high praise.

Then we, too, joined, and sang aloud,
    " Glory to God most high,
The Father, Son, and Comforter,
    To all eternity!"

And thoughts arose of those we love,
    Whose footsteps with us trod
Along the path of life awhile,—
    Then mounted to their God

They scaled the golden steps to heaven,
    And passed the inner gate;
We in the outer Church remain,
    Nor understand their state.

We know not the new song they sing,
    Save that they sometimes cry,
"Unto the Lamb that once was slain
    Be praise and majesty!"

And we may join—though at our prayers
    On earth no more they bend;
In adoration of the Lamb,
    Our voices still can blend.

O Thou of whom the family
    In heaven and earth is named,
For whom such joys Thou hast prepared,
    That Thou art not ashamed

To call us "brethren," and to let
  Our souls through anguish learn
To love, as Thou dost, patiently,
  Without the glad return

From voice of answering love, without
  The help of sense or sight:—
Sustain us, when we faint and fail,
  Till we are purgèd quite

From all alloy of earth and self,—
  Till we are meet to be
Gathered at last with our beloved,
  Thy countenance to see.

Submission.

THE conflict, Lord, is ended, and Thy grace
    Hath now the victory won,
And taught me thankfully to say,
    "Father, Thy Will be done."

I scarcely understand how the wild storm
    Thus suddenly should cease;
How the long buffeting should end
    In unexpected peace.

Once it seemed very hard that Thou shouldst choose
    What I had loved the most,
To make me say, "Thy Will be done,"
    At such a bitter cost.

But now I see that it was wisest Love,
    Claiming its rightful throne:
That in my consecrated heart
    Thou mightest reign alone.

SUBMISSION.

My soul is crowded all with silent thoughts,—
    A hush I cannot tell;
Like the strange pauses in a dream,
    One motion may dispel.

What though the Future with its unknown depths
    Be hidden from my sight,
I know that its untrodden paths
    Lead onward into light.

Yes, I will trust Thee: Thou didst once on earth
    Carry our griefs alone;
Thou soughtest comforters to help,
    And friends, but they were gone.

Thou knowest all my need: upon Thy care
    I utterly depend;
Thy patience, that has borne the past,
    Will keep me to the end.

Passing Hence.

THOU'RT passing hence, O pilgrim soul!
   Thy mortal vest lay down;
Robe thee with immortality
   And glory for a crown.

O lonely, lonely anchoret,
   Cloistered in Sorrow's shrine,
When thou dost reach thy Father's Court,
   What welcome shall be thine!

Though gloomy shadows have been long
   Brooding above thy tent,
The lovely light begins to dawn,
   The night is almost spent.

What though thy lamp burn fitfully,
   Flickering high and low,
It, with the oil of gladness filled,
   Again in heaven shall glow.

The silver cords are breaking fast
  In that fond lyre-like heart,
Yet in heaven's glorious melodies
  Its music shall bear part.

Turn up the hour-glass yet once more,
  Swift as that falling sand,
Thou'rt passing through the wilderness,
  Unto the Holy Land.

The secret cross of Baptism,
  Invisible till now,
Is turning to a glory star
  Upon thy dying brow :

And Hope, endiademed with light,
  Holds thee unto her breast,
While Love, with her angelic wings,
  Is folding thee to rest.

On through the toilsome desert way
  Our footsteps still must roam,
But joy to thee, Belovèd One,
  For thou art going home.

Chastisement.

I HAVE been dumb, and held my peace,
    Because the stroke was Thine:
When Thou dost bare Thy holy Arm,
    Omnipotent, Divine,
Shall mortal man, corrupt within,
Complain that Thou dost visit sin?

Thou didst it, Lord! This sorrow came,
    Obedient to Thy Will:
Thy hands have made me; Oh! in wrath
    Remember mercy still.
I will be silent at Thy awful throne;
Lord, Thou hast fashioned me: Thy Will be done.

Thou didst it;—Thou Whose heart of love
    Was wounded first for me:
Thou didst endure this life, and bear
    Death's deepest agony.

How can I murmur or complain,
When Jesus suffered grief and pain?

Thou didst it;—Who art watching now
　　Each pang and heavy sigh:
Yes, I submit, if only Thou
　　Wilt hold me, and stand nigh:
I will not struggle with the knife
That wounds me, but to save my life.

Thou didst it, Who art gone on high,
　　Where many mansions be,
There to prepare a glorious Home,
　　And deathless friends for me:
Shall I rebel against the love,
That fits me for my Home above?

Ah no! e'en through this load of fears,
　　My heart is springing up,
To thank Thee for the boundless grace,
　　That overflows my cup.
But I am weak, and cannot always say
"Thy Will be done:" remember I am clay.

Put a new song within my lips,
  And let my spirit sing:
I give Thee up my inmost heart,
  Saviour, and Priest, and King;
Take to Thee, there at least, Thy power, and reign;
Henceforth, "to live is Christ, to die is gain."

Retrospect.

I SOUGHT to praise Thee, but my heart
    Went heavily along;
It seemed too weak with sorrow's smart,
    To lift itself in song.

I sought to count Thy mercies o'er,
    To view them one by one,
But sighed o'er what may be no more,
    Chief blessings that are gone.

Till I am brought to worship now,
    E'en for this very grief;
To praise the mercy with which Thou
    Hast kept back all relief.

That while I struggled and rebelled,
    Thou didst in love go on
Did'st take that which I tightest held,
    And set my heart upon.

That Thou didst lead me into gloom,
    Far from the light of earth,
To show me it was but a tomb,
    And death my better birth.

And when, enthralled by earth, I see
    Those who in childhood's days
Gathered the buds of hope with me,—
    A deep, deep thrill of praise

Echoes along my heart, that I
    Am now beside Thy Cross,
Longing, by faith, with Thee to die,
    And count the world but loss.

Thus in Thy presence now I kneel,
    Filled with one deep desire;
One strong ascending hope I feel
    Glow like celestial fire,

That Thou wilt unto me impart
    Thy truth on every side,
To pour o'er my corrupted heart
    Its renovating tide.

Hide nothing from me that Thy power
  Can make my soul to know,
And from that knowledge cause, each hour,
  A holy love to grow.

O draw me close unto Thy breast,
  Close as my soul can come,
And let me there take up my rest,
  In my eternal Home.

The Pilgrim.

PILGRIM, where goest thou?
      "Unto the shrine
And presence of my Lord, a Prince Divine
And wearily upon mine arm I bear
A freewill offering to meet Him there."
    Surely, 'tis precious, if 'tis fit to bring
Unto so mighty and so rich a King.
Tarry a moment, let me look within
Upon thy treasure:—why, 'tis marred by sin!
Here is a bottle almost full of tears,
Bundles of heartless prayers, and faithless fears,
Talents grown rusty with long lying by;
A half-strung harp, whose music is a sigh:
Necklaces strung with vows that once were fair,
But broken now, or spent in empty air;
Thoughts, feelings, passions, all with evil rife:
Neglected duties, and a wasted life:—
All that is here, thy Lord will surely spurn,
Except, perchance, this little closèd urn

Of Love; yet that defilèd is, and small:
O hapless Pilgrim, this is not thine all?
   "All, gentle Stranger; yet I do not fear
But that my Lord will in His mercy hear
My earnest prayer, and will be pleased to take
This worthless offering, for His own dear sake:
One great Oblation on His Altar lies,
One perfect and sufficient Sacrifice;
And for the sake of that one precious Name,
A full acceptance now all suppliants claim:
I fain would give my heart, but it hath been
Stolen by the world away, and so my Prince,
Who with His searching eyes the theft hath seen,
Hath sent to me His gracious Spirit since,
To say that He the wanderer will find,
And new create it after His own mind,
Then lay it on His Altar; there to be
Filled ever with the oil of His felicity."

Still Waters

THOU didst despise the quiet flow
    Of day succeeding day,
In undisturbed tranquillity
    Whiling thy life away.

A home was thine, all calm and true,
    Bright with affection's smile,
But after earth's magnificence
    Thy proud heart yearned the while.

Thou didst refuse the daily round
    Of useful patient love,
And longedst for some great emprise
    Thy spirit high to prove.

Peace had been thine, couldst thou submit
    To duty's fixed employ,
But thou didst turn aside to weep
    For overflowing joy.

So a change came:—a few short days,
  These were enough to bring
A shadow, that for ever took
  The brightness from thy spring.

Few as they were, they were enough
  To bid thy rest depart,
To wake a fountain deep and strong
  Of grief within thy heart.

Now thou hast learnt to prize the flow
  Of day succeeding day,
In undisturbed tranquillity
  Whiling thy life away.

Thy Future now is not on earth:
  Christ teaches thee to soar
To where the living waters glide
  On an eternal shore.

The forms of beauty and of power,
  That here thy heart controlled,
Are all developed for thee there,
  In a diviner mould.

When meek obedience thou hast learnt,
　In silence, and unknown,
Thou shalt do perfect service there,
　In presence of the Throne.

The joy that would have held thy soul
　Enchained by time and sense,
With Heaven's high interest shall be given,
　Thy lasting recompense.

Thou shalt be changed:[a]—a few short days
　Will be enough to bring
A glory, that through heart and flesh
　Shall breathe immortal Spring.

[a] 'We shall all be changed.'—1 Cor. xv. 51.

A Contrast.

STEDFAST, gentle, self-forgetting,
   Patient, tender, brave and wise,
Bounteous as the dew of morning,
   Nobly free from all disguise;
Thrilling like a harp responsive
   To each touch of lofty thought,
And true-hearted to remember
   The least kindness for thee wrought·
Brighter and more ardent spirit
   Never on this fair earth trod;
Such thou art amid thy fellows;—
   But oh! what, unto thy God?

Cold beneath His touch as marble,
   Dark and silent as the grave,
Careless, selfish, and ungrateful,
   Scantly serving like a slave;
Scorning the bare thought of yielding
   Unto Him thy heart, thy health,

A CONTRAST.

Grudgingly and meanly giving
  Of thy time and of thy wealth;
Living freely on His riches
  As thine own, by night and day,
And yet haughtily refusing
  By His Will to rule thy way.

Pause, O blinded, and consider
  How it is these things can be:
Then unto thy patient Saviour
  Turn thee, on low bended knee:
Tenderly He calls and seeks thee,
  With a long and anxious quest,
Yearning ever to enfold thee
  Joyfully unto His breast:—
Love Eternal for thy coldness
  Doth not from the search depart,
But still follows, pleading meekly,
  "Child of earth, give Me thine heart."

From His glory He descended,
  For thy sins to mourn and die;
Then from out the grave returning,
  He ascended to the sky;

Whence He poureth out His Spirit,
    Offering to thee gifts untold ;—
Of these marvels now thou hearest
    With unloving heart and cold !
Noble, gentle, self-forgetting,
    In earth's best affections rife,
There is yet one thing thou lackest—
    'Tis the Spirit's breath of Life.

Self-Accusation.

IN the white robes of His Priesthood,
   On the Mediator's Throne,
Christ receives each one who cometh
   His transgressions there to own.

Thou *must* meet Him in the Judgment,
   In His awful power arrayed;
To Him first, as Intercessor,
   Be thine inmost life displayed.

E'en to half-reluctant suppliants
   Meekly He inclines His ear,
Catches every broken utterance,
   Every moving pulse of fear.

If for words too much bewildered,
   If thou dare not seek His face,
Silent lay thy heart before Him,
   He will understand its case.

Only long to be delivered
  From each remnant of disguise
Only let Him lay in ruins
  All thy refuges of lies;

Only strive to say, "My Saviour,"
  As thou liest at His feet;
He can from thy dust and ashes
  Spotless holiness complete.

Through the new strange stillness round thee,
  Through the palpitating air,
A new dawn will steal upon thee;
  How, thou canst not tell, nor where.

Piercèd hands will touch and bless thee,
  Words descend from highest heaven,
Breathing through thy heart's recesses,
  "O My child, thou art forgiven!"

Disappointment.

ALL round the rolling world, both night and day,
A ceaseless voice ascends from those who pray:
"Thy Will be done on earth, as now in heaven;
Unto our souls a perfect choice be given."

All round the rolling world, both night and day,
A ceaseless answer comes to those who pray:
By shattered hopes, crossed plans, and fruitless pains,
Thy heavenly Master thine allegiance trains.

Guessing some portion of His great design,
Thou seek'st to forward it by ways of thine:
He Who the whole disposes as is meet,
Sees a necessity for thy defeat.

Yet to the faithful there is no such thing
As disappointment; failures only bring
A gentle pang, as peacefully they say,
"His purpose stands, though mine has passed away."

All is fulfilling, all is working still,
To teach thee flexibility of will;
To great achievements let thy wishes soar,
Yet meek submission pleases Christ still more.

When Love's long discipline is overpast,
Thy will too shall be done, with His, at last,
When all is perfected, and thou dost stand,
Robed, crowned, and glorified at His Right Hand.

"Upbraideth not."

"God . . . upbraideth not."—St. James, i. 5.

RECEIVE me, Lord; to Thee I fly,
    Defeated and dismayed,
Thou only Refuge from the sound
    Of voices that upbraid!

There is no day, from out the past,
    But has its bitter cry,—
No friend, but I may sometime read
    Reproaches in his eye.

E'en those for whom my wealth of love
    Outran their utmost need,
Might say, "Why, with intenser prayer,
    For me didst thou not plead?"

Nature, through every changing mood,
    Has a low chiding tone,
Telling of uncompleted works,
    And of occasions flown.

The very Father of all lies
    Speaks truth, as he recalls
Transgressions, failings numberless,
    Infirmities and falls.

Conscience, imperious grown, reproves
    The evil I have wrought:
My wishes, purposes, and life,
    Are baser than I thought.

Exhausted by the tumult wild,
    And overborne, I pine
For silence, infinite in depth
    Of tenderness Divine.

Against Thee only have I sinned,
    And all this evil done;
Yet Thou alone dost not upbraid,
    O meek and spotless One!

No weak reproaches full of self
　　Thou makest me endure,
For stronger even than my sin
　　Is Thy great power to cure.

Thou wilt do all I have undone,
　　Re-make what I have marred,
My foolish hindrances the while
　　Wilt gently disregard:

And when Thy work is all complete,
　　Then Thou wilt call it mine,
And I shall hear Thee say, " Well done!
　　Henceforth My joy is thine."

The Annunciation.

STRAIGHT from the presence of the Lord of
    heaven
  The Angel Gabriel speeds upon his way,
To where, beyond the mountains of Judæa,
  The dwelling of a Hebrew maiden lay;
And as a sunbeam that in silence steals,
He seeks the chamber where the maiden kneels.

Silent he stands, his hand a lily holding,
  That through the air celestial fragrance flings,
Bright figure, and soft shadow, showing strangely
  Against the background of his large white wings;
His head, in love and reverent wonder bent
Towards her, for whom this embassy is sent

The morning sunlight lay upon her forehead,
  The morning breezes stirred her floating hair;
Her earnest eyes were raised to heaven, as seeking
  The Object of her deep adoring prayer—

The unseen, eternal, and immortal King,
Who man's lost heritage again will bring.

Whom will He send to earth as its Deliverer,
   The great Messiah of the chosen race?
When will the tardy hours bring round His Advent,
   What mother shall receive that crowning grace?
When will the strife, the wrong, the woe be past,
And David's Son ascend His throne at last?

Hushed is the prayer, yet the fair lips are parted
   In deep amazement at her angel-guest,
Whose gleaming presence gently dawns upon her:—
   "Hail, Mary! thou of women the most blest:
God will redeem the promise that He gave;
His Son of thee takes flesh, the world to save."

Humbly she hears the thrilling words of wonder,
   And yields herself to the all-perfect Will—
His only, His for ever, a fair temple
   Which His Divinity doth form and fill:
"Behold, I am the handmaid of the Lord:
So let it be, according to Thy word."

Still Mary kneels; for over soul and body
    The o'ershadowing grace is streaming in full flow,
While deep within, beneath her heart's quick pulses,
    The Life of heaven and earth begins to glow:
And He by Whom all wrongs will be redrest,
In a few months will lie upon her breast.

O Christ, our King! the King and Son of Mary,
    Our Champion, Saviour, Brother, Priest, and Friend!
Teach Thou each yearning throb of hero-worship
    How to pass on to Thee, as its true end:
Let every gleam of light that charms our eyes
Lead us to Thee, from Whom it took its rise.

Over these hearts, so prone to harbour idols,
    Let the o'ershadowing grace for ever stream,
Until the Son has been revealed within us—
    Our Hope of glory, and its fairest dream;
Until we know Thee, not by angel's tongue,
But as our Life of life, Whom we shall see ere long.

The Divine Infancy.

HOME of the Christ-child at Nazareth,
   Let my thoughts within thee dwell;
There,—where, shrouded in man's weakness,
   Dwelleth Light Ineffable!

Angels circle round adoring,
   Watchful, as the hours go by;
As the mystery advanceth
   Of that wondrous Infancy.

Cradled by a human Mother,
   Though with grace Divine imprest,
Playing with soft aimless touches
   On her cheek and on her breast.

In the water from the fountain,
   'Mid the oleanders wild,
In the early morn and evening,
   Mary bathes the unsullied Child.

When the soft blue veins show clearer
  In the water's liquid gleam,
Oh! how little thinks that Mother
  Of the pure life-giving stream,

That a Gentile spear shall open
  In that gracious, tender side,
For the healing of the nations,
  For a Covenant world-wide.

Joyfully she clothes and feeds Him,
  And she trains Him day by day,
Till the beautiful Child Jesus
  Has been taught to kneel and pray.

Humbly were the small Hands folded,
  Bended was the golden Head:
But God only, in the heavens,
  Understood the prayer He said.

For of all the cries and pleadings
  That have yet ascended there,
None has ever come before Him
  Mighty as that Infant's prayer:

'Twas the highest act of homage
  That the world had ever shown;

And the purest pulse of worship
  That man's heart had ever known.

Then He learned to be obedient;
  And with simple, winning grace,
In the precincts of that cottage
  He has filled a child's true place.

And the name at which Archangels
  Bow adoring, and say "Lord,"
In that peasant-home was spoken,
  As a common household word.

Saviour! by Thy cradle kneeling,
  I with shame my pride confess;
By Thy Holy Incarnation
  Cleanse me from its bitterness.

In Thy life I would be hidden;
  From self-seeking let me cease;
Breathe upon me from Thy Childhood
  Its unutterable peace.

As my spirit ripens onwards,
  Let it take the mould of Thine;
In Thy lowliness abiding,
  In an infancy divine.

"He laid His Hand upon Me."

Lay Thy Hand upon me
    When I fall asleep,
Through the silent hours
    Close beside me keep;
Then the Prince of Darkness,
    Ruler of the air,
Will not dare to touch me,
    If Thy Hand is there.

Lay Thy Hand upon me,
    Tenderly restrain
All too eager longings,
    Every impulse vain:
Calm my spirit's chafing,
    Restless with long care;
Murmurs melt in silence
    When Thy Hand is there.

Lay Thy Hand upon me,
    When I rashly stray

Into paths forbidden,
  Choosing my own way.
Ah! how much correction,
  Lord, I have to bear,
Yet must take it meekly,
  For Thy Hand is there.

Thou didst lead a blind man
  In Thine earthly days,
Didst lead him long and gently,
  And show him light's pure rays:
Oh! through all life's journey,
  To its furthest strand,
Surely he remembered
  How he clasped that Hand.

Lead me now and always,
  Even to the last,
Till the way is ended,
  And the darkness past:
Till I reach the glory
  I was born to share—
This its crown and centre,
  That my Lord is there.

Bethany.

SIX days before the Passover,
   The blessèd Saviour came
To Bethany, where He remained
   Until His hour of shame;
His last abode was in the home
   Of Lazarus, His friend;
Those He had loved while in the world
   He loved unto the end.

The shadow of the Passion lay
   Brooding on all around,
Though what it meant they could not know,
   Its depth was too profound
For mortal eye to search it out,—
   Though woman's love might see
Further than most into the cloud
   Of that great mystery.[a]

[a] St. Matthew, xxvi. 12

His sacred Heart in its lone depths
　　Was heaving at the thought,
That human nature's perfectness
　　Through suffering must be wrought.
And yet He set His face to go
　　With firm endurance on,
And rose above the nature weak
　　That clothed the Eternal Son.

And He did then for evermore
　　That form of trial bless,
If only sinking hearts to Him
　　Will turn in their distress;
One ray of glory in the crown
　　That on His brows is set,
Is drawn from those deep pangs of fear
　　He never can forget.

Not for Himself alone He fears:
　　That all-foreseeing Eye
Distinguishes each single throb
　　Of human agony.
He wept o'er every closing grave
　　Unto the end of time;

His soul drank in the rising swell
   Of Sorrow's awful chime.

He took full measure of the grief
   Of every separate saint,
As, one by one, each on his cross
   Must tremble and grow faint;
He knew, though He had given them rest,
   They first must find sore strife,
Must seek e'en through the gates of Death
   His promised gift of Life.

Yet even then His joy arose,
   For ever to increase,
In knowing that this suffering host
   Would find in Him their peace;
The travail of His soul might bow
   That sacred Head to earth,
Yet He is satisfied to see
   The new Creation's birth.

He feels the presence of meek love
   Already at His side,
The gentle ones who cling to Him,
   And breast the world's strong tide;

He sees the eyes that to Him turn,
  The hands that seek His own,
Those who, in sharpest discipline,
  Trust Him, and Him alone.

Apostles, Martyrs, the long line
  Of royal, warrior souls,
Flash on Him their triumphant smiles
  From where the Future rolls;
The white-robed multitude, whom none
  Can number or declare,
Waft Him their floating voice of praise
  Already on the air.

Lord! since our griefs on Thee were laid,
  And Thou hast felt their sting,
Help us in holiest calm to take
  Our turn of suffering;
Thou didst look on unto Thy joy,
  And so by grace will we,
But we would clasp Thy Cross, and feel
  We owe that joy to Thee.

Good Friday.

COLD as the snow
   On mountain range,
That all the summer's glow
   Can never change,
My heart remains,
   E'en while I kneel,
And muse upon those pains
   Which Thou didst feel!

A dim amaze,
   A dull, dead woe,
As on thy Cross I gaze,
   Seems all I know.
O could I be
   Contrite indeed!
Could I but truly see
   I made Thee bleed!

O Lamb of God!
   O Crucified!

Down on the blood-stained sod
  My face I hide.
I cannot take
  The mystery in;
But, Saviour, let it make
  Me free from sin!

Free from its guilt, —
  Yes, that I know:
Thy blood, that there was spilt,
  Doth overflow
The whole world's sin; —
  Atones for all:
But here, here, deep within,
  Let Thy blood fall!

Upon these stains,—
  This feeble will,
These paralysing chains
  Of former ill:
And if not yet
  My tears o'erflow,
O make me sternly set
  Sin to forego!—

All doubtful things,
   Soft, subtle snares,
To which the weak soul clings,
   And, clinging, shares
The Serpent's heart,
   That feeds on dust,
And does the Serpent's part,--
   Betrays the Just.

Lord, I am Thine:
   Let this Thy Cross
Evermore keenly shine
   O'er gain and loss!
For it must win
   My heart, my all:
Oh! deeper yet within,
   Let Thy blood fall!

Woman's Commission.

St. John, xx. 17.

WHEN, upon Easter morn,
    The risen Saviour came
To Mary, as she kept
Beside His grave, and wept,
    He called her name.

Without one shade of doubt,
    Her heart replied, "My Lord!"
The mystery received,
Of Life through Death achieved,
    Her faith adored.

Unto that perfect faith
    Christ gave at once employ;
Not to embrace His feet,
In trance of rapture sweet,
    But—nobler joy!—

To publish the great fruits
  Self-sacrifice had borne—
Christ risen, rising still;
Proclaiming, by His Will,
  To hearts that mourn:

" Go, say that I ascend,
  Unto My Father's throne,—
My Father, and *My* God,
Your Father, and *Your* God:
  Not Mine alone."

O Woman, take thy stand
  Upon this high position,
And faithfully hand on,
Till Death itself is gone,
  This great Commission.

The Apostolic Line
  No higher message bear;
They who the world must roam,
And thou, within thy home,
  One glory share.

Teach it thy brother's soul,
  By full unselfish love,
By consecrated youth,
By lips of stainless truth,
  Hopes fixed above.

Throned on thy husband's heart,
  Whisper the message there;
And let him all around,
Within home's guarded bound,
  Breathe heavenly air.

And let the risen life
  Beating within thy breast,
Cradle the sleeping boy,
In a deep hush of joy,
  Laid there to rest.

Yea, teach the saving truth
  To every son of thine,
His passions to control,
To waken in his soul
  The Life Divine.

And lonely ones as well,
　　With all your untold store
　Of love still garnered in;
　To spend it, O begin! —
　　Give Christ your store.

Wherever human hearts,
　　In high or low estate,
　Waste upon earth and sense
　Hopes that should soar from thence,
　　Your work doth wait.

Behold, it lies outspread;
　　In Christ's strength then arise;
　Fix on the misery round,
　The sin that doth abound,
　　Pure, fearless eyes.

To you the Voice still speaks ·
　　"Go, say that I ascend
　Unto My Father's throne,
　(Yours, and not Mine alone,)
　　His Gift to send."

O Woman! then work on
　Beneath thy Saviour's eyes:
Thy joy is yet to come;
Thy peaceful perfect Home
　Is in the skies.

Day-Break.

St. John, xxi.

THE night is dark, and this long toil
    Not yet has reached its close:
Faint and disheartened, my soul longs
    For light and for repose.

The heaving sea, the moaning wind,
    They toss me to and fro;
My net hath swept all round my bark,
    But yet no spoil I show.

The past possesses me:—my sins
    In all their shame appear;
Ungrateful, cowardly, and vain,
    Myself I hate and fear.

Shall I be always thus, and fall,
    When highest good I seek,
With love so passionately strong,
    Yet treacherously weak?

He knows my love; He has forgiven:
　But can He make me whole?
He raised the dead, but can He give
　Life to a dying soul?

It seems a dream, that He has been
　Once more amongst His own,
That we have heard Him breathing Peace,
　In that familiar tone.

Then *is* there conquest over death,
　And victory o'er the grave?
And will He henceforth have all power
　In heaven and earth to save?

O that I knew where I might find
　His place of dwelling now,
And, kneeling under those pierced Hands,
　Renew each broken vow!

He draws me, wins me; I am His;
　Yes, His whom I denied!
Perchance He yet may let me dare,
　And suffer, at His side.

These baffling mists and blinding spray
    Hang cold upon my brow;
Yet the day breaks, the shadows fall
    Outstretched behind me now.

And dimly on the distant strand,
    Just touched with morning light,
I see a Form—now half revealed,
    Now shrouded from the sight.

There is a banquet on that shore;
    A voice says, " Come and dine;
Yea, feed on Me, and fill at last
    That longing heart of thine."

The yearning deepens, strengthens, swells;
    Success cannot beguile;
That which through life I've toiled to win,
    Seems worthless, by His smile.

I come, I come—though cold the waves,
    Though steep the shore may be;
I come—from earth, from death, from self,
    To be made one with Thee.

Ascension Day.

AT the Name of Jesus
   Every knee shall bow,
Every tongue confess Him,
   King of Glory now.
'Tis the Father's pleasure
   We should call Him Lord,
Who from the beginning
   Was the mighty Word.

Mighty and mysterious,
   In the highest height,
God from Everlasting,
   Very Light of Light!
In the Father's bosom,
   With the Spirit blest,
Love, in Love Eternal,
   Rest, in perfect rest.

ASCENSION DAY.

At His voice, Creation
  Sprang at once to sight,
All the angel faces,
  All the hosts of light;
Thrones and dominations,
  Stars upon their way,
All the Heavenly orders,
  In their great array.

Humbled for a season,
  To receive a Name
From the lips of sinners,
  Amongst whom He came;
Faithfully He bore it,
  Spotless to the last,
Brought it back victorious,
  When from death He passed.

Bore it up triumphant,
  With its human light,
Through all ranks of creatures.
  To the central height;
To the Throne of Godhead,
  To the Father's breast,
Filled it with the glory
  Of that perfect rest.

ASCENSION DAY.

Name Him, brothers, name Him,
    With love as strong as death,
But humbly and with wonder,
    And with bated breath:
He is God the Saviour,
    He is Christ the Lord,
Ever to be worshipped,
    Trusted, and adored.

In your hearts enthrone Him!
    There let Him subdue
All that is not holy,
    All that is not true.
Crown Him as your Captain,
    In temptation's hour;
Let His Will enfold you
    In its light and power.

Brothers, this Lord Jesus
    Shall return again,
With His Father's glory,
    With His angel train:
For all wreaths of empire
    Meet upon His brow,
And our hearts confess Him,
    King of Glory now.

"The Lord and Giver of Life."

*"No man can say that Jesus is the Lord, but by the
Holy Ghost."—1 Cor. xii. 3.*

JESUS, our Lord and King! Ah! pause and see
   Whose power it is by which we homage give:
For Pilate wrote upon the accursèd tree
   In royal style, that Name by which we live.

Are there not Pilates evermore, who say
   "Lord, Lord," and crave to see some deed of might,
Who will not learn His Will, nor yet obey,
   But crucify the silent Lord of Light?

Those blessèd Feet that walked Gennesaret's waves,
   Soon after trod the blue elastic air,
And mounted where the sapphire glory paves
   The Throne which He will worship now, and share.

But who shall comfort, now that He is gone,
   And keep in our remembrance what He taught;
Moulding our acts as He would have them done,
   Cleansing the springs of action and of thought?

Ten days passed on before the answer came,
    Ten slow expectant days, of ceaseless prayer ;
Then a swift rushing wind, and tongues of flame,
    The Presence of an unseen Power declare.

He Who of old within the triple Life
    Of the Eternal Godhead moved and wrought,
And from earth's darkness, and chaotic strife,
    A world of perfect good and order brought ; —

He Who by perfect fellowship abode
    In the humanity of God's own Son,—
From Heaven descends, mysteriously endowed
    With power to help and heal us, one by one.

He is the Spirit of the Son indeed,
    Co-equal in humility and love,
In that strong patience, which can mourn and bleed,
    But never, from the soul it loves, remove.

For eighteen hundred years has He remained,
    Quickening, transforming, working as He will ;
Quenched, scorned, forgotten, limited, and pained,
    He, in His meekness, lingers with us still.

All growth in wisdom, all pure love's increase,
   All noble daring, and endurance meek,
All battles for the truth, all sighs for peace,
   The presence of the Comforter bespeak.

We seem divided, scattered, and alone;
   The tranquil heavens with sounds of discord ring:
Meanwhile He binds us all and every one,
   In bands of growing union, to our King.

We pray for holiness, then deeply sin;
   Now we presume, then angrily despair:
He bears our wilfulness; He pleads within,
   Unuttered moans, that never thrill the air.

His Breath, too, stirs all prayer, that doth rejoice
   To rise like incense to the central Sun;
All praise is the intoning of His Voice,
   Swelling from whispers in the heart begun.

O Spirit of our spirit, Life's pure Fount!
   True Friend of the true Bridegroom whom we wait;
Reveal Him clearer to our souls, that mount
   With keen expectance towards their promised state.

'Tis not enough that He our place prepares,
   With beauty infinite adorns our Home,
And by the power of His unceasing prayers
   Prevails, that those He loves shall thither come.

We would be like Him, Whom we call our Lord
   We would reflect the Image that we love:
O chasten our whole being, to accord
   With the deep tides of life that in Him move!

Thou gracious Spirit! Comforter most meek!
   As Christ His glory veiled in flesh of man,
So Thou Thy Godhead dost conceal, in weak
   Blind spirits, who Thy working cannot scan.

But when He comes for Whom we hourly pray,
   And we are one with Him, in heart and mind,
He will unfold to us the wondrous way
   In which Thy Love, and His, for us combined.

Till then, we yield ourselves in deepest trust,
   Into Thy hands, their impress to receive;
We would adore Thee, humbled to the dust:
   O Holy Ghost, we do in Thee believe.

Hide Me.

HIDE me, Lord, for I am weary,
    Weary of the world's hard ways;
Of its foolish blame and wonder,
    Of its yet more foolish praise.

Men will judge with blind half knowledge,
    Though Christ said, "Judge not at all:"
Let Thy glance of perfect insight
    Now upon my spirit fall.

Men must work with noise and clamour;
    Thou dost work in silence sweet:
For awhile Thou hast withdrawn me,
    To lie quiet at Thy feet.

Hide me from the mists of error,
    In my own vain heart that rise;
From its fears and perturbations,
    From its selfishness and lies.

HIDE ME.

Hide me in the time of sorrow,
   When each nerve is on the strain;
Compass me with loving-kindness,
   When Thou scourgest me with pain.

Hide me from the craft of Satan,
   From his kindling breath of flame,
From his arrowy temptations,
   Sent with an unerring aim.

Be Thou close at hand to hide me
   When the hour of death draws near;
When I tremble to be parted
   From the flesh, that veils me here.

Hide me, in Thy mercy hide me,
   Till I once have seen Thy Face;
Then, my Saviour, then unveil me,
   As a faultless work of grace.

In the presence of Thy glory,
   Safe for ever at Thy feet,
I, at last, shall hold communion
   With the souls I yearn to greet.

O what joyful revelations
  Of enduring, patient Love!
O what infinite expansion
  The long-guarded heart shall prove!

Blending, melting, in each other,
  Without let, or thought of fear;
All the hindrances there vanished
  Utterly, that hold us here.

With full insight understanding
  Thy great work within each soul,
New varieties of glory
  Every history will unroll.

Soaring through the golden ether,
  Piercing it like shafts of flame,
Rise the notes of adoration
  To the Source from whence they came.

As the Prayer of prayers is answered,
  "I in them, and Thou in Me;"[*]
Perfect all, in One, for ever—
  Trinity in Unity.

[*] St. John, xvii. 23.

The Love of God.

GO back to the beginning,
    And then back earlier still;
Trace the first forms of being,
    In the Creator's Will;
And find there thine own image,
    What thou wast meant to be;
Conceive of the perfection
    Which He designed for thee.

From out the Life Eternal
    Time sprang forth as a stream,
Time rolling ever onwards,
    Thy life begins to gleam:
Where now is that fair image
    That lay in God's deep thought?
Behold it, marred and altered;
    Behold what thou hast wrought!

O weak, and false, and wilful!
    O cold, and stubborn heart!
Self-centred, and self-seeking,
    Neglecting thy true part
In the well-ordered working
    Of God's unerring ways;
Thy origin forgetting,
    The purpose of thy days.

Who now shall find a healing
    For this deep-seated ill,
And who shall bend and strengthen
    This weak and crooked will?
Who grapple with the darkness
    And agonies, that lie
Hid in the righteous sentence,
    "The soul that sins shall die?"

Love now has changed its action,
    And suffering and decay
Brought in among the creatures
    Who wandered their own way;
Love hides itself in sorrow,
    Draws us with links of pain,
And wearies us with sadness
    To drive us home again.

THE LOVE OF GOD.

Look back along the ages;
   Behold on Calvary's crest
Thy crucified Creator —
   Thy God, by sin opprest —
Seeking His lost Creation,
   The souls whom He had made:
He came as Man among us,
   And was by man betrayed.

The sins of all the sinful
   Were heaped upon His Head,
As He, on that high Altar,
   In expiation bled,
And reconciled the creatures
   To Him who loved them still,
And offered to the Father
   A faultless human Will.

O Holy, Holy, Holy,
   I flee unto Thy breast;
Upon its stainless justice
   Let a lost sinner rest!
By Mystery o'ershadowed,
   By boundless Love constrained,
I yield myself adoring,
   For glory to be trained.

Now Thou art in my nature,
    More mine, than is my sin,
Fulfil me with Thy Presence,
    And make all new within!
Let body, soul, and spirit,
    Be so indwelt by Thee,
That of Thy life within me
    They may the organs be.

Then, through a few more struggles,
    Through a few dying years,
From weakness, pain, and darkness,
    From loneliness and tears,
From doubts and deep abasement,
    Perplexities and loss,
Forebodings, sinkings, anguish,
    Faint shadows of Thy Cross,—

Lead me to Thy great Future,—
    To my appointed place,
In Thine accomplished purpose
    Of Glory and of Grace;
In Thy renewed creation,
    Brighter than ere its fall,
Where Thou wilt reign for ever,
    And Love be all in all.

The Cross.

SINK in, thou blessèd sign!
    Pass all my spirit through,
And sever with thy sacred touch
    The hollow from the true.

Sorrow shall wear thy badge,
    As her fair sign of hope;
No self-indulgent voice may say
    That grief must have full scope.

Sickness shall own thy sway,
    With stedfast patient eye,
Thoughtful for others, who must bear
    The weight of sympathy.

Thou shalt restrain my soul
    'Mid the world's tempting gloss:
Schemes, wishes, memories, all must feel
    The burden of the Cross.

The understanding high
    Shall bow beneath thy might,

Relinquishing its vain attempt
    To gauge the Infinite.

Through my heart's very ground
    Thy ploughshare must be driven;
Till all are better loved than self,
    And yet loved less than Heaven.

And my impatient will
    Under thy yoke shall learn,
How to be constant to one end,
    Yet yield at every turn.

On vanity and sin
    Stamp thy broad bars of shame:
High was my birthright, but my life
    Deserves no meed but blame.

Draw thy clear cutting lines
    In scorn above my pride,
And keep me, with meek wounded heart,
    Close to the Crucified.

Oh! can it, must it be,
    That thou wilt rule all thus?
The Cross to Jesus was no dream:
    Shall it be so to us?

In Pain.

BY Thine anguish cleanse my soul,
By Thy Passion make me whole;
Weak and helpless on the Tree,
Thou didst gain the victory:
Weak and helpless as I lie,
Thou canst triumph, sin can die.

Search me through, and nothing spare,
Burn the sin out that is there,
All that is of Thine and Thee
Quicken into energy.
Let Thy Love enlarge my heart,
Deepen, soften every part.

In the silence deep and still,
Bind me closer to Thy Will;
Earthly friends are far away,
Be Thou with me night and day:

Earthly happiness I miss,
Make me conscious of Heaven's bliss.

Teach me how to guess aright,
Of the wonders out of sight:
Let my spirit grow more clear,
Heavenly whispers let me hear:
Let the veil become more thin,
And the glory pierce within.

Make me pure, that I may be
Able to be one with Thee,
And reveal Thyself, for Thou
Art the thing I long for now.
When the veil at last is riven,
To behold Thee will be Heaven.

Holy Communion.

SAVIOUR, above all heavens ascended high,
With Angels and Archangels waiting nigh,
Yet still a wounded Lamb upon the throne,
Still with a human heart, remembering Thine own.

O Priest! O Victim! who Thy prayer dost pour
For me, as for the ransomed gone before,
Grant me by faith that Sacrifice to see,
And thus my whole heart, Lord, to offer up to Thee.

Pour out Thy Spirit on Thy Church below,
Where Thy forgiven children humbly bow;
Thou whom no limit and no bound can hold,
The secret of Thy Presence unto us unfold.

Thine all-obedient Life, Thy Death, we plead;
Upon the Sacred Elements we feed:
We mourn that night, whence most our healing springs,
When thirty silver pieces bought the King of Kings!

HOLY COMMUNION.

Man sold Thy Life for money mean and small;
To ransom man, the Saviour gave His all:
We hide our faces,—would our hearts might break,
As, prostrate at Thy Throne, the gifts of Love we take!

O Love Omnipotent! this will of mine
Shall yet obey Thy gentleness Divine:
Death and Hell fall before Thee; none may say
Where Love will pause upon its all-victorious way.

Thou know'st I cannot love Thee as I would,
But yet abide with me, my only Good!
The evening of my days is hastening on,
The journey of my life must now be well-nigh done.

The way is desert, difficult, and long,
Temptations thicken, and the foe is strong;
All is tumultuous and perplexing here;
Draw up my heart where undivided Truth shines clear.

To the Church Catholic that is at rest,
In Thine own Glory perfected and blest;

Whatever darkness on our path may be,
They hold bright fellowship with the Eternal Three.

In spirit let me share their full repose,
Their calm pure heart, in which Thine image glows;
Their blissful hope of joys more glorious still,
Their deep complacency in Thine all-holy Will.

I know Thee, Saviour! walking at my side;
Through earth's last shadows be Thou still my Guide:
Then, calm as ripples dying on the strand,
Be my transition to the undefilèd Land!

The Net.

IN the outskirts of the Kingdom,
   Toiling amidst lowest things,
God doth educate the spirit,
   Searching out its inmost springs.

Common things have gathered meaning;
   All are charms of heavenly power,
By His shaping, who from evil
   Causes purest good to flower.

Words Divine, and Prayers, and Blessings,
   Sorrows, Sacraments, and Alms,
Humble souls, with care o'er-wearied,
   Bended knees, and folded palms;

These are working wondrous changes,
   Unperceived, except by faith,
Gathering for the eternal Harvest
   Life from out the mass of Death.

These their wondrous web are casting,
   Unperceived, in the deep sea,
In whose meshes float unheeding
   Those who fancy they are free;

Till the strong sure hand of power
   Draws them on unto the shore;
Lord! Thy Net cannot be broken,
   We are Thine for evermore.

Associations.

OUR hearts are overcharged with memories sweet,
    Of those whom we love best:
Why are the memories so slow to rise,
    Of Him, earth's dearest Guest?

We know the story, old yet ever new,
    Of how He came to save,
And dwelt as Very Man with brother-men,
    From childhood to the grave.

And earth has tokens manifold and fair,
    Which He has touched with light;
Memorials of his blessèd Presence throng
    For ever on our sight.

Our chequered human life, our daily food,
    The flowers along the way,
And all the glorious and the common things,
    That meet us day by day.

From the first early flush of rosy dawn,
    To midnight's solemn skies;
From the young carols of the opening Spring,
    To where the Autumn sighs;

From the fair tender form of infant life
    We in the cradle lay,
To where beside the bier of manhood's strength
    We cast ourselves to pray;

Thoughts of the Christ should rise at every turn,
    And hold us all day long:
Alone, or when in crowds, each heart should hear
    That blessèd under-song,

Which upon Nature's harp is whispering still
    Its soft undying strain,
Moving the wakeful soul with deep desire
    To see His Face again.

O hear it, ye, on whom His gracious Hand
    Has made the sacred sign,
The Cross of Suffering,—who have meekly bowed,
    To bear that brand Divine;

For pain and weakness make Him to our hearts
    Nearer and dearer seem,
Till life becomes a story, sweet though sad,
    Of which He is the theme.

Night.

HOW heavily the evening lies,
  On aching limbs and sleepless eyes,
And as the day gives place to night,
The spirit seems to lose its light.

The Past breaks loose upon the soul,
Oppressing it beyond control;
While thickly, from the Future, glare
Visions of anguish and despair.

Conscience, and Fancy,—thoughts of all
That most can harass, and appal,
A strange tumultuous vigil keep;
And only Hope and Reason sleep.

O troubled heart! O fevered head!
There watches One beside thy bed,
Calmer than moonlight on a flower,
Stronger than Satan's wildest power.

He knows the Night, Who made it pass
At first, like breath from gleaming glass,
When at His word, "Let there be Light,"
The day-spring flashed, and all was bright.

He knows it, Who on mountains bare
Passed its long hours in lonely care,
Kneeling beneath the Syrian sky,
Pleading till dawn with the Most High.

The hurrying night-wind round Him beat,
The driving sea-foam swept His feet,
As forth He walked upon the wave,
The tempest-tost to cheer and save.

He knows the Night, Who felt its power
Of darkness, in that evil hour,
When the betrayer's torchlight shone
On silver olive and grey stone;

The flight of friends, the wrath of foes,
The weight of sin, fear's sharpest throes,
The Accuser's voice, the cruel storm
Of scourging on that wearied Form;

The utter shame, the Gentile's scorn,
Denial base, the crown of thorn,
The fiercest strain of Satan's might,—
These came upon Him in the Night.

He searched the Darkness through and through;
Its gloom, for Him, has nothing new,
As night by night He turns us round,
Into the shadowy outer bound.

There, when afflicted and alone,
O call upon that Mighty One!
And hold Him fast, and make Him stay,
And bless you, till the dawn of day.

Remember, Night has mercies too;
Its pains are only for the few;
Think upon all the peace it brings,
Folding soft creatures in its wings.

As wearily you toss and sigh,
Thousands of infants sleeping lie,
And man, and beast, and bird, and flower,
Grow stronger, for the midnight hour.

And if the darkness had not been,
We never should the stars have seen,
Or guessed that the clear azure sky
Veiled myriad worlds, that rolled on high.

Then spend no more dark hours alone,
But call upon the Mighty One;
And hold Him fast, and He will stay
Until the shadows flee away.

The Sea Shore.

THE sea lies like a mirror,
    All full of golden light,
With streaks of purest chrysophrase,
    And veins of silver bright:

The silent ships go swiftly,
    And leave no trace behind,
The white sails spread and quiver,
    Before the gentle wind;

There floats one little vessel
    Just close upon the strand,
And eager crowds before it,
    In expectation stand;

So floated once a vessel
    On such a glassy sea;
And so a crowd once gathered
    Of old in Galilee.

For He, Whose voice had drawn them,
   Taught them from out the ship,
And all that throng hung breathless
   Upon His eye and lip.

And still, the words He uttered
   Can make hearts throb, and burn·
We still are waiting for Him;
   When, when will He return?

When the world's lawless evil
   Has reached its highest tide,
Then will the Veil star-spangled
   Draw its blue folds aside.

Then the doors everlasting
   Lift up their heads again,
That He may be revealèd,
   Whose right it is to reign.

"O come!" our hearts are calling;
   "O come!" all nature cries—
The green earth's expectation,
   The sea's incessant sighs.

Dying.

WHY will ye call it "Death's dark night?"
Death is the entrance into Light:
Behind its cloudy purple gates
The everlasting Morning waits.

Then fear not Death, its pains, its strife,
Its weakness—these belong to life:
Death is the moment when they cease,
When Christ says "Come," and all is peace.

Once, in the silence of the night,
A maiden lay with smiles of light,
Her blue eyes gazing open wide,
And a few violets by her side.

Her mother asked her why she smiled,
What pleasant thoughts the time beguiled?
She answered her with gentle breath,
"Thoughts of the sweetness found in Death."

Death was but as her dark-hued flowers,
Exhaling sweetness through the hours,
Till, ere the early dawn could be,
She breathed into Eternity.

Waiting.

LORD of my nights and days!
    Let my desire be,
Not to be rid of earth,
    But nearer Thee.

If I may nearer draw
    Through lengthened grief and pain,
Then, to continue here,
    Must be my gain;

Till I have strengthened been,
    To take a wider grasp
Of that eternal Life,
    I long to clasp;

Till I am so refined,
    I can the glory bear,
Of that excess of joy,
    I thirst to share;

Till I am meet to gaze
    On uncreated Light,
Transformed, and perfected,
    By that new sight.

Sorrow's long lesson o'er,
    Death's discipline gone through,
Thou wilt unfold to me
    What Joy can do.

Glad souls are on the wing,
    From earth to Heaven they flee:
At last, Thine hour will come,
    To send for me.

Reveal the mighty Love,
    That binds Thy Heart to mine:
Thy Counsels, and my will,
    Should intertwine.

Lord of my heart and hopes!
    Let my desire be,
Not to be rid of earth,
    But one with Thee.

Paradise.

ONE cry of mortal anguish,
    And then the Cross He leaves,
While Paradise the blessèd,
    The Conqueror receives;
That bright and tranquil region
    For Christ has waited long,
And now He treads its portals,
    Head of a glorious throng.

Then welcomed Him, rejoicing
    The souls of all the just,
Who, from the world's creation,
    Have died in hope, and trust;
Then Eve's deep expectation
    Was satisfied indeed,
And Abraham beheld Him,
    The long-desired Seed.

Since then, a countless number,
    Soul rescued after soul,
Have passed unceasing upward,
    Unto the heavenly goal:
New forms of varied beauty,
    But all made like their Lord,
The sweet and full-toned chorus
    Of that one primal chord.

All holy ties of kindred
    There blend and merge in one—
The children of the Father,
    Accepted in the Son.
Earth's long processions ending,
    There form in circles vast,
There meet the first and latest,
    Where Time is overpast.

They are at one for ever,
    In love intensely keen,
With memories cleansed, yet perfect,
    And joy where shame has been:
Their prayer now knows no languor,
    Their praise unceasing flows,

From rapture, that still higher
And more abounding grows.

Their language is too mighty
To be translated now;
The great Apostle heard it,[a]
Yet could not make us know
The glory of its meaning,
The music of its tone;
But panted for the hour
When it should be his own.

Panted for the "far better,"[b]
The far, far better Land,
The presence of Christ Jesus,
The joys at His Right Hand:
For he had seen that region,
While yet in mortal guise,
Guest in the many mansions,
The homes of Paradise.

---

[a] "He was caught up into Paradise, and heard unspeakable words, which it is not lawful (possible) for a man to utter."—2 Cor xii. 4.

[b] Phil. i. 23.

O think of that assembly!
  Their beauty and their peace;
Souls perfect, yet receiving
  Love's infinite increase.
In full illumination,
  Knowing as they are known,
The transitory ended,
  And the imperfect flown.

Henceforward, and for ever,
  They live, live unto God;[a]
He is their source, their object,
  Their light, and their abode.
As sea-flowers in the ocean,
  As white clouds in the air,
He forms them and expands them,
  Is round them everywhere.

His joy is through them spreading;
  His Will, their will sustains;
Joint heirs, in rich possession,
  Of Christ's eternal gains.
With vision all unclouded,
  They see Him face to face,

[a] St. Luke, xx. 38.

Share in His intercessions,
    And ministries of grace.

They rest from all their labours,[a]
    Yet serve Him day and night:
Their earthly forms are sleeping,
    But they, in deep delight,
Wait for the Resurrection,
    Of Life the perfect Crown,
The time of Restitution,
    Christ's triumph, and their own.

From henceforth, saith the Spirit,
    Write, " Blessed are the dead ;"—
Believe that in Christ's Kingdom
    All change must higher lead:
And when, in bitter anguish,
    You close some tender eyes,
Doubt not they are beholding
    The King of Paradise.

[a] Rev. xiv. 13.   [b] Rev. vii. 15.

The Redemption of the Body.

OUT of the dust, God formed man's flesh, to be
  Deathless, and fair;
Man sinned; his robe of innocence was gone,
  And left him bare:

Exposed to every form of misery,
  Disease and pain,
Till, when Death's cruel work is done, he turns
  To dust again.

Death reigned, supremely, tyrannously strong,
  Four thousand years;
The generations of mankind went down
  Mid hopeless tears.

At last, there fell a sound through the night air,
  The Heavens were stirred:
But on the dull deaf earth, only a few
  Poor shepherds heard.

The sky was gleaming with the wondrous light
    Of a strange Star;
But only three wise men perceived it there,
    And came from far.

Yet ne'er before did such mysterious night
    Enshroud the earth;
For in it, this poor sinful race received
    A second birth,

When, in the feeble dying flesh of Man,
    A Babe forlorn,
The Life that from Eternity had been,
    In Time was born.

So Christ became Death's subject, e'en as we,
    And freely gave
That sacred, sinless Body to the Cross,
    And then the Grave.

Death triumphed, and believed that on the Cross
    Life's Sceptre broke:—
But Christ arose, and Death for evermore
    Must wear His yoke;

No tyrant now, but servant, whose chief task
    Is to unbind
The chains, by which the children of the King
    Are here confined:

For since Christ's Body rose from out the Tomb,
    And sought the skies,
So the whole race of man, now joined to Him,
    Like Him must rise.

Oh! false ungrateful words, to call the Grave
    Man's long *last* Home!
'Tis but a lodging, held from week to week,
    Till Christ shall come.

It is a store, of which Christ keeps the key,
    Where in each cell
Are laid, in hope, the vestments of the souls
    He loves so well:

And when He comes, upon His marriage morn,
    In light arrayed,
He will invest His own in those same forms,
    All glorious made.

O Saviour of the Body Mystical—
  Of flesh and blood,
Which cannot enter into Life, but through
  Jordan's dark flood—

Save us, for we are Thine by bond and pledge:
  To Thee we trust
That which we hold most precious, when we say,
  "Dust unto dust."

Gathered Flowers.

RING out, sweet Flowers, from your blue shining bells,
  The hidden fragrance of the deep green dells;
While, mingling with each fresh and woodland tone,
Come lights and shadows from Life's spring-time flown.
The body may in chains of weakness be,
But the unfettered Fancy still is free;
Free to roam out along a thousand ways,
Where the wind travels, and the sunlight strays:
To wander after each gay breeze that calls,
And leap with all the leaping waterfalls,
Or dream enchanted, as the soft air stirs
A sea-like murmur in yon belt of firs.

Shall we complain, if for a little while
He hides us from the light of Nature's smile?
If, held apart within some silent room,
Sore pain or weakness curtain us with gloom?
It is but that our souls may nearer grow
Unto the Heart whence Nature's glories flow.

O Heart of Jesus! whence all flowers have birth,
Whence come the sweet sounds of this lovely earth,
And birds have beauty, and young things their mirth:
O Heart! whence the Baptismal waters flow,
And the celestial Food by which we grow,—
That fills all chalices with that true Wine
Which maketh glad the heart, with health divine,
And is the sad soul's only Anodyne,—
Thou through Thy riven side hast made a way
For wanderers to return, who widely stray;
For chiefest mourners to obtain relief,
Who gaze on Thy diviner depth of grief,
For Light and Immortality to come,
Bright as the Spring flowers, from their winter tomb.

Lord, if Thy Wounds have filled the world with peace,
What shall Thy Joy do, when all sin shall cease,
And the new earth shall yield her full increase!

After Dark.

THERE'S a sighing in the poplars,
    As the clouds of evening weep,
And a sadness and a shiver
    Upon my spirit creep:
For all that makes up summer
    Is now so quickly flown;
The short days die so early,
    And darkness settles down.

But I'm waiting for the Morning
    When the light shall come again,
The pure and perfect shining,
    That cometh after rain;
The bright and blessèd Morning,
    When I shall wake refreshed,
And in immortal garments
    Shall royally be dressed.

I have been so impatient
   To gain a higher state,
And have asked my Lord to help me;
   But He always answers "Wait."
And I know He must be wisest,
   Who would have me love Him best;
And at last I shall be contrite
   When I sink upon His breast.

But my lamp will burn so dimly,
   Though I trim it up with care;
It seems almost extinguished,
   In this heavy midnight air:
And waiting makes me sleepy,
   And faint with hope deferred:
What if I am not ready,
   When the sudden cry is heard?

Yet I'm longing for the Morning
   When the marriage bells shall ring;
For the great shout and the trumpet
   That shall proclaim our King;
For the flight of utter rapture,
   To meet Him in the air,

For the band of radiant faces
   That I know will all be there.

     *   *   *   *

Sigh then, ye winds of autumn,
   Ye clouds of autumn weep,
And let a passing sadness
   Across my spirit sweep.
What though my life's short summer
   Is all too quickly flown,
What though the days die early,
   And darkness settles down :—

I am waiting for the Morning
   When the light shall come again,
The pure and perfect shining
   That cometh after rain ;
For that transcendent Morning,
   When I shall wake refreshed,
And in immortal garments
   Shall royally be dressed.

Home.

"HOME, home," she cried exulting,
    "Death is a glorious Birth,"
Then gently slipped her shackles,
    And sprang away from earth:
The Angels caught her softly,
    And bore her up the steep;
The gold gates closed behind her,
    And we remain to weep.

Ah! would she so advise us,
    Could she lean from out the blue?
And that sweet voice steal o'er us,
    Refreshing as the dew?
"Weep ye that I have entered
    My Father's House above,
And, resting from all sorrow,
    Am perfected in love!"

"Beside my grave, O weep not!
  Nor say I'm lying there;
Turn up your faces heavenwards,
  Into the sun-lit air;
Think how I'm far above you
  In 'Everlasting Spring,'
In the Imperial City,
  And presence of the King."

"Lost in His light of glory,
  For which He made me meet,
I rest in adoration
  Down at His sacred Feet;
From the wasting of long sickness,
  From the weariness of life,
From throes of helpless pity,
  And the useless din of strife;"

"From the burning shame of finding
  A traitor deep within,
From battles long with error,
  And struggles fierce with sin,
From the haunting of sweet voices,
  That through my spirit rang,

From walking in waste places,
   And life's long hunger-pang;"

"From wounding misconstructions,
   From unappeasèd claims,
From unsuccessful labours,
   From disappointed aims,—
From all these He has freed me
   By His victorious Hand;
Will not ye, too, then hasten
   To this Immortal Land?"

"The trumpet note of Welcome
   Is always on the blast,
It has no time to die away,
   The souls come in so fast:
Then faint not ye, Belovèd,
   But let hope conquer sorrow,
These golden gates shall open
   To let you in to-morrow."

Uselessness.

BEWAIL not thou thyself with restless haste,
  Nor say, God lets thy life run all to waste.
Thou hast thyself to master, and subdue:
No easy work, methinks, for thee to do.
For His own Court, God will thy soul prepare;
And jewels for the Crown are cut with care.

Say not, all useful work thou art denied:
Behold, Christ's Censer waiteth at thy side,
He, in compassion, lets it down to thee;
Heap on thine incense, heap it full and free.
  Pray for thy Friends: that every deed of love
May be received and registered above;
Kind words, and patient ways, and soft regards,
All turned in heaven to stores of rich rewards.
Pray for the Sick, who suffer in all lands,
God's prisoners, laid in bonds by His own hands:
That on them all His likeness He would trace,
And grant them special offices of grace;

That they, through languor, may not cease to care
For occupations they no longer share;
But that by prayer, and sympathy, and smile,
The burdens of the weary they beguile.
For kind Physicians plead—that as our Lord
Trusts them with works of healing, at His Word
Each one may bring to Him his own sick soul,
To be by Him forgiven, and made whole.

Pray for crowned heads, with all their weight of care;
For broken hearts, and all the sorrows there:
For widows, orphans, solitaries, wives,
For heartless homes, where Love nor lives nor thrives:
That all the women of this English land
May be a stedfast, noble, saintly band,
Seeking, in all, less to be great than good,
Fashioned after God's type of womanhood.
Remember Statesmen, and all master minds,
Priests, Poets, Teachers, Rulers of all kinds;
That all Christ's Messengers be channels true,
'Twixt us and God, with Whom we have to do:
That they may choose the right—nor fear the strong,
And from base love of Mammon crown the wrong.
Plead for the wanderers from Christ's fold who stray,
For those who know it not, nor know the way:

For the whole race which He has made His own,
For which He intercedes before the Throne.
All useful work, O heart! art thou denied,
While this great Censer waiteth at thy side?
Heap on thine incense, heap it full and free;
He, when He offers it, will think of thee.

Thou art too weak to pray?—then, spirit, rest:
Lie where Saint John lay, on thy Master's breast;
He knows thy weakness, understands each sigh,
The yearnings of thy heart, its voiceless cry.
A child who knows not why, nor whence its pains,
But meekly lies, and frets not nor complains,
Is as a dewy flower, that breathes at even
A perfume sweet, into the heart of Heaven.—
Lie childlike thou, and ask not whence, nor why;
Lie still, and hear thy Saviour's lullaby.

Rest.

O JESUS Merciful! bend down
   In Thy compassions deep,
As sleepless and alone I lie,
   And watch beside me keep.

There is a holier, sweeter rest,
   Than the lulling of this pain;
And a deeper calm than that which sleep
   Sheds over heart and brain.

It is the soul's surrendered choice,
   The settling of the Will,
Lying down gently on the Cross
   God's purpose to fulfil.

For this I need Thy Presence, Lord,
   My hand held close in Thine:[a]

[a] Isa. xli. 13.

Infuse now through my spirit faint,
    An energy divine.

Feed me with Love, imprint on me
    Thine awful kiss of Peace:
Let me be still upon Thy Breast,
    Nor struggle for release.

And sanctify my weakness, Lord;
    Nature's extreme distress
Is just the time when it may learn
    God's glory to express.

Stamp in, O God, at any cost,
    The likeness of Thy Son!
Filial submission to Thy Will
    Is heaven itself begun.

Offerings.

LORD, I had planned to do Thee service true,
To be more humbly watchful unto prayer,
More faithful in obedience to Thy Word,
More bent to put away all earthly care.

I thought of sad hearts comforted and healed,
Of wanderers turned into the pleasant way,
Of little ones preserved from sinful snare,
Of dark homes brightened with a heavenly ray;

Of time all consecrated to Thy Will,
Of strength spent gladly for Thee, day by day,—
When suddenly the heavenly mandate came,
That I should give it all, at once, away.

Thy blessèd Hand came forth, and laid me down,
Turned every beating pulse to throbs of pain,
Hushed all my prayers into one feeble cry,
Then bid me to believe, that loss was gain.

And *was* it loss, to have indulged such hopes?
Nay, they were gifts, from out the Inner Shrine,—
Garlands, that I might hang about Thy Cross,
Gems, to surrender at the call Divine.

As chiselled image unresisting lies
In niche by its own Sculptor's hand designed,
So, to my unemployed and silent life,
Let me in quiet meekness be resigned.

If works of Faith, and labours sweet of Love,
May not be mine, yet patient Hope can be
Within my heart, like a bright censer's fire,
With incense of thanksgiving mounting free.

Thou art our Pattern, to the end of time,
O Crucified! and perfect is Thy Will;
The workers follow Thee in doing good:
The helpless think of Calvary, and are still.

Weariness.

O PAIN perpetual! wearing strength away,
    While spirits flag, and fail,
And all the many-coloured hues of life
    Have faded, and grown pale.

O thoughts unwedded to the deeds ye seek!
    Life that all fruitless seems —
Long dull inaction, yet without repose;
    All feeling, fear, and dreams!

'Tis thine infirmity, impatient soul:
    Remember now the years
That are at God's right Hand, and cast away
    Thy grievances, and fears.

Think of the infinite abyss of peace
    In which thy lot shall be,
Where ages are but ripples that run o'er
    Eternity's deep Sea.

WEARINESS.

Give thou God leisure to prepare thee for
    That destiny sublime,
When e'en with lifeless things His Hand works on,
    Unheeding space and time.

Listen! borne inland from the rocky coast,
    Comes the wild voice of waves,
Which for uncounted centuries have toiled
    Among the deep sea-caves.

This ray, from yon fair star serenely bright,
    Now broken in thy tears,
Had travelled onwards, ere it reached thine eyes,
    For sixty thousand years!

When times and spaces of such vast extent
    Before thy thoughts combine,
Into a momentary pang shrinks up
    This long, long pain of thine.

Then, if thy weary heart recoils, and faints
    At such high wondrous ways,
Turn where the great Creator bears a life
    Which thou canst count by days.

A few hours' Agony, the Bloody Sweat
    From that shrunk Form has wrung;
And a few more have brought Him to the Cross,
    To die when He was young.

Strive thou in soul to sympathize with Him,
    The infinitely great;
For He has stooped to understand, and share,
    The weakness of thy state.

Give thanks; the Lord is patient; He will work
    A perfect work in thee:
And grudge no time to make thee fit to bear
    Joy for Eternity.

Good Night.

GOOD Night, Good Night, the dreams of earth are ended,
    Its glory and its passion passed away,
And a new sense, of joy and terror blended,
    Holds all my heart in its resistless sway:
The things of Time are fading from my eyes,
The Unseen encircles me with strange surprise.

When I look back upon the way I've wandered,
    The wasted energies, the time mis-spent,
Wealth, hopes, affections, all too often squandered,
    That might have been to Heaven before me sent,
My strength is turned to weakness at the sight;
The time for toil is past: Good Night, Good Night.

There is one only hope for souls repenting,
    With heart and work, alas! all incomplete;
It is the Cross, which spans both worlds, presenting
    A pathway sure for the most feeble feet;

I see it now, outspread in all its might;
Who trusts that Bridge is safe: Good Night, Good Night.

Prepare me then, Beloved, the Food Immortal,
   To strengthen me upon my wondrous way,
And go thou with me to the furthest portal,
   To which companion footsteps yet may stray;
Then hide thine eyes, with their soft pleading light,
For I depart alone: Good Night, Good Night.

Let those dear lips yet once, once more caress me,
   Then pause awhile until the Morn shall come;
For when with eager joy again they press me,
   'Twill be within our Father's House, our Home,
Among His gathered children, pure and bright,
Within the Land where there is no more Night.

Gone Before.

GONE, gone — but gone before!
   Silent thy name
Upon the lips where once
   Its music came.

Now the sweet cadence falls
   On heavenly air,
Angels are sounding those
   Syllables fair.

Gone, gone — but gone before!
   No tears can rise,
To dim the light of those
   Immortal eyes.

Nevermore cloud can pass,
   Or stain endure,
Upon thy soul redeemed,
   Perfect and pure.

K

High amid star-like saints,
    Radiant and calm,
Girded with golden harp,
    Bearing green palm :

Bend from the battlements
    Thy shining brow;
O thou Belovèd One,
    Watch for me now !

Almost I see thee, thou
    Seemest so nigh,
When I look trustfully
    Up to God's sky ;

To the pale tender blue,
    Rippled all o'er,
With the ribbed cloudlets, like
    Sands on a shore.

Oh ! could I drive my bark
    In on that tide,
Leap on the golden sands,
    Spring to thy side !—

They who are one in Christ,
    Hid in His heart,
Death cannot sever, nor
    Hold long apart.

Soon they clasp hands again,
    All partings o'er,
Where the Life-Giver has
    Gone on before.

Death.

O MOURNERS, call not that a Home,
    Over whose threshold Death can come!
Call it a sacred shrine for prayer,
A sphere for love, and duty fair,
A place in which to train Man's heart
For sympathy to do its part;
But oh! wherever Death can come,
In mercy call not *that* a Home.

Yet Death is kinder than of old,
E'en though he still must rob the fold:
He stands beside the quiet Dead,
Points an entire life outspread,
A character in all complete,
A written history most sweet,
That we may muse upon it well,
And to our sinking spirits tell
How faith and hope had guided on,
Until the latest fears were gone;
Until God's Image was displayed,
And saintly Patience perfect made.

Death's final seal is deep imprest,
On thoughts and memories so blest;
It can be only when we slight
The value of their tender light,
And of their onward guiding ray,
That we can e'er refuse to say,
Although it be with failing breath,
" O fearful and yet gentle Death !
Take from us our Beloved away,
We would not, could not, bid them stay,
None other can teach love like thee,
Love to endure eternally."—

Joy too, Death's Angel brings to light,
Unto the purged and stedfast sight.
Oh ! not for mighty temples planned,
Or finished work by Genius spanned,—
Not for the lights of sunset skies,
Glories o'erflooding heart and eyes,—
Not for a long desired birth,
Or for that fairest lot of earth,
When equal hearts in union blest
Are met for evermore at rest,
Can we rejoice with joy so pure,
So calmly certain to endure,

As when an unrepeated sigh,
Then a deep stillness brooding nigh,
Tells that the unchained soul has flown
There, where before her prayers had gone,
Home, from this scene of grief and wars,
Home, blue and high, beyond the stars.
Then, strong in patience, we can wait,
E'en at the Grave's unclosing gate,
While, deep within, Death plants our seed;
For we are then most sure indeed,
That Spring's bright day will bring the hour,
When our immortal plant shall flower.

Sad and faint-hearted! Courage then!
And struggle on like earnest men;
Those closed and seeming sleeping eyes
Are watching you from out the skies.
The Past—into God's sight is gone,
The day now Present—fleeteth on;
What of the Future?—O my King,
The endless Hallelujahs ring
Within the Home that Thou hast found,
Where Love and Life at last are crowned!

Desolation.

" But THOU remainest."

O GOD, this grief is more
    Than I can bear alone.
My heart seems suddenly to have become
    A cold crushed stone—

Till, touched with rapid shocks
    Of Memory's keen pain,
It plunges in strong agony, to fall
    Down cold again.

Lord, why such cruel wrath,
    Hard to be understood?
How can it be that it is sent in Love?
    That Thou art good?

I am so new to pain,
  To gloom and to despair;
Where is the heart on which my life has leaned,
  O where? O where?

For this world, all is lost;
  Blessings and gifts may come,
But all my happiness has passed away
  Into the tomb.

Ah, no!—not in the tomb!
  Forgive my want of faith!
Thou know'st how hard it is to grasp the thought
  Of Life through Death.

It was not *him* they left
  In the grave's cloister sealed:
That was his shadow—*he* had soared away
  Where welcomes pealed.

He is at rest with Thee;
  And though no tidings come
From out that region very far away,
  It is our Home.

Yes, yes, he is with Thee—
    But Thou art with me too;—
Then must the distances that 'twixt us lie
    Be very few.

Come, then, poor struggling heart,
    Give thyself up to God!
Gaze back into the Man of Sorrows' face!
    Tread where He trod!

Along His Royal road
    Of consecrated grief,
Which He endured unto the Cross for us,
    Nor found relief.

Saviour, beneath that Cross
    In helplessness I cling,
Trusting no more to arm of flesh, but now
    Be Thou my King.

O keep me close to Thee,
    When the quick shifting throng
Of earthly cares oppress my heart and brain;
    For Thou art strong.

Be with me when I faint
  Beneath my weight of woe;
For Thou the secret mysteries of grief
  Alone dost know.

Hold me through life, through death,
  Until to Thee I come;
For Thou wilt show to me the path of life:
  Thou art my Home.

Self-Dedication.

CLOSE those white eyelids—kiss them—then obey:—
Duty's behests must meet with no delay;
Lay down thy memories, thy hopes most fair,
And let the Past be all extinguished there;
Extinguished for a moment, but to rise
Bright and immortal, in Love's native skies;
Extinguished for a moment, that thy pain
May die for ever, and pure joy remain.

Look up! Heaven's gate upon its silent hinge
Is quickly closing—yet a gleaming fringe
Of Glory edges the still open door;
Send in thine heart—swift—and for evermore.
Be His alone, Who died to win thy love;
Be His, all His, Who pleads for thee above:
Work with Him meekly as His hands unwind
The tangled web, that Earth has round thee twined;
Work for Him truly in Life's daily task,
And what the future hides, nor fear nor ask;

Seek His Will only — leave to Him the rest,
And toil or suffer, as shall please Him best.

Look onwards! — Hush! — the Marriage is complete,
The banquet is prepared, the Virgins meet:
The Angels' snowy, opal-tinted wings
Are folded, and the Harpers hush their strings,
As stands the Bridegroom, Conqueror, King, and Priest,
To pour His benediction on the Feast.
The Bride, adoring, thinks upon that hour,
Ere her Lord gave Himself to Death's dark power,
When at that Passover He lifted up
His eyes to heaven, and having given the Cup,
He said: "O Father, I Thy work have done,
"Into Thy glory now recall Thy Son:
"I will that she I ransom as My Bride
"Be with Me, in My glory at Thy side." [a]
And the strong might of that prevailing Prayer
Has brought her to His Throne and Glory there;
Uplift the trumpets, wake the harpstrings now,
And let the voice of many waters flow.

[a] St. John, xvii. 4, 5, 24.

On an Infant's Grave.

SOFT, soft and tender, be the sorrow,
    Tears full of sunlight o'er the ground
Wherein that infant form lies sleeping,
    A short sleep, till the Trumpet sound.

It is the light of Heaven that hides him;
    Life, and not Death, has come between:
O Christ, there lieth in Thy bosom
    A baby that in ours has been.

He will grow up among the angels,
    Upon "the hidden manna" feed,
And by the streams of living waters
    They will his tender footsteps lead.

Weep on! but let it be for gladness,
    Tears full of sunlight o'er the ground
Wherein that infant form lies sleeping,
    A short sleep, till the Trumpet sound.

A Little While.

MY silence and my solitude
    I offer up to Thee.
Lord, where the glad Hosannas sound,
    Wilt Thou not think of me?

Oh! many the foundations are
    Of Thy fair City tall,
And many are the gates of pearl
    Set in the jasper wall.

And many are the Mansions there,
    And many are the feet
Upon the jewelled pavements, where
    The saved and happy meet.

A little while, and shall I be
    One of that radiant throng?
A little while, and shall I join
    Their everlasting song?

A little while,— O throbbing heart,
    Then surely thou canst wait
A little while, and learn to be
    Serene, though desolate.

Thanksgiving.

YET one more strain of joy and triumph holy,
   For a new work achieved and victory won ;
Another vessel in the Haven anchored,
Another warfare well and nobly done.

Yet one more flag is on the ramparts floating,
Yet one more footstep on the Crystal Sea,
Another harp has joined the " many waters,"
Another soul, the Kingdom of the Free.

O Lord our God, we give Thee thanks unfeignèd,
For our Beloved who walk with Thee in white,
E'en though our path below must now be shaded
By heavy clouds, that hide them from our sight.

And, Lord, that love which Thou hast given us for them,
We weeping offer, to be kept on high,
Until the Day when we shall worship with them,
Entranced amid the splendours of the sky.

Teach them to love us now, with heavenly fulness,
To pray for us, who in this desert roam;
O send them to the threshold to receive us,
When we, too, go to dwell with Thee at home.

And shall we see each radiant face reflecting
The light that to Incarnate Love belongs?
And hear those voices, rapturously blending
With thousand times ten thousand angel-songs?

But oh! not now; yet, yet awhile we linger,
Till weaned from life's uncured idolatry,
Till with unfaltering truth our hearts can whisper,
"Whom have we, Lord, in all that heaven, but Thee!"

Alpha.

BE Thou my Alpha! Other Lords than Thou
    Erewhile have ruled this sinful soul of mine,
But now I wholly turn to Thee, and say,
        Lord, I am Thine.

Thou *art* my First, O Lord!—my highest choice!
My will has yielded to Thee, and found rest;
By many a token sure Thou teachest me,
        I love Thee best.

When evening clouds hang clustering round the sun,
And sad sweet memories make my heart their prey,
It swells again exultant at the thought
        Of that great Day,

When Thou wilt come with clouds, that shall have caught
New and surpassing glories from Thy light;
The light that then shall rise for evermore,
        Nor sink in night.

And Music, in its mystery and power,
That erewhile would have steeped my heart in tears,
Now breathes a promise through its aching depths,
    Of those bright years,

That are at Thy right hand in Joy's own home,
Where the eternal Anthem never dies,
But ebbs and flows, where Music's hidden spring
    In Glory lies.

All Nature, that before seemed one deep dream
Of beauty, steeped in sorrow, now doth ring
With earnest voices of expectant joy,
    That call their King.

O wounded but undying Love! we feel
Thy veilèd Presence is amongst us here:
Unto the longing eyes that seek Thee now,
    Shine out more clear:

Rule me, my Lord! that love may be confirmed
By glad obedience, and by service due;
Let me be pliant underneath Thy Hand,
    Meek, docile, true.

Alpha and Omega.

ALPHA and Omega!
    Be Thou my First and Last:
The Source whence I descend,
The Joy to which I tend,
When earth is past.

Open my waking eyes,
And fill them with Thy light;
    For Thee each plan begun,
    In Thee each duty done,
Close them at night.

Enfold me when asleep;
Let soft dews from above
    Refresh the long day's toil,
    Wash off the worldly soil,
And strengthen love.

Men speak of Four Last Things;
Death, and the Judgment Hall,
   Hell, and the Heaven so fair:
   But Thou, O Lord, art there,
Beyond them all.

There is no "last" with Thee,
But·only our last sins,
   Last sorrows, and last tears,
   Last sicknesses, last fears;—
Then Joy begins:

Joy without bound or end,
Concentric circles bright,
   Spreading from round Thy Throne,
   Flowing from Thee alone,
O Love! O Light!

Lay Thy right Hand of Power
In blessing on my brow;
   Heaven's keys are in Thy Hand,
   Its portals open stand;
I fear not now.

Lead Thou me gently in,
Thou Who through Death hast passed;
   Then bring me to Thy Throne,
   For Thee I seek alone,
My First and Last.

THE REMAINING VERSES ARE ADDED

AT THE

REQUEST OF SOME FRIENDS.

Memorials.

THIS life is but a school-time,
    In which we learn to love
The friends we see around us,
    The unseen God above.

Some learn by active service,
    Others, in grief and pain;
Some seem to reap in gladness,
    The rest, to toil in vain.

The great thing is, to study
    To seek our Lord in all:
His great Love to remember,
    Whatever may befall.

We know the blessèd story,
    Of how He came to save,
And lived as Man amongst us,
    From childhood to the grave.

And Earth has now her tokens,
　　That He has touched with light;
Memorials of His kindness
　　Are ever in our sight.

The Pillows ᵃ that we rest on,
　　The Hairs ᵇ upon our head,
The Bason ᶜ of clear water,
　　The Towel ᵈ fair outspread:

Our raiment of White Linen,ᵉ
　　The Well ᶠ beside the way,
Our Basket ᵍ and our Money,ʰ
　　Our Children ⁱ at their play:

The little sparrows ʲ feeding,
　　The Wind ᵏ that strews the grain,
The Shepherd ˡ gently leading
　　His lambs along the lane:

St. Mark iv. 38.
St. Matt. x. 30.
. St. John xiii. 4, 5.
ᵈ Ibid.

ᵉ St. Luke xxiii. 53.
ᶠ St. John iv. 6.
ᵍ St. John vi. 13.
ʰ St. Luke xx. 24.

ⁱ St. Matt. ii. 11, &
　　xviii. 2.
ʲ St. Matt. x. 29.
ᵏ St. John iii. 8.
ˡ St. John x. 14.

The patient Ass [a] at labour,
    The Cattle in the stall,[b]
The Cock [c] at morning crowing,
    The Dove's [d] voice at nightfall:

The gleaming of the Fire [e]
    Whose warmth is round us spread,
The broiled Fish [f] and the Honey,[g]
    The little Loaves of Bread: [h]

The Boats [i] upon the Water,
    The Fishers [j] on the shore,—
These things remind us of Him,
    These, and a hundred more.

And Stars [k] are all the dearer,
    For that one wanderer bright,
That shone of old at Bethlehem,
    Upon the Wise Men's sight.

---

[a] St. Matt. xxi. 2.
[b] St. Luke ii. 7.
[c] St. Luke xxii. 60, 61.
[d] St. John ii. 16.
[e] St. John xxi. 9.
[f] St. Luke xxiv. 42.
[g] Ibid.
[h] St. John vi. 11.
[i] St. Matt. xiv. 32.
[j] St. Luke v. 2.
[k] St. Matt. ii. 9, 10.

The jewelled lights of Sunset,[a]
　　The glory of the Dawn,[b]
The snowy Clouds[c] of Heaven,
　　The Flowers[d] upon the lawn:

The wild Sea's[e] tossing splendour,
　　Of green and crested waves,
The firmly planted Mountain,[f]
　　Its silent rocky Caves:[g]

The voice of Sighs and Weeping,[h]
　　The Bier[i] where lies the Dead,—
These speak to us of Jesus,
　　Of words that He has said.

And pain and weakness make Him
　　Nearer and dearer seem,
Till life becomes a story
　　Of which He is the theme.

---

[a] St. Matt. xvi. 2.
[b] St. John xxi. 4, & Rev. xxii. 16.
[c] Acts i. 9.
[d] St. Luke xii. 27.
[e] St. Mark vi. 48.
[f] St. Luke vi. 12.
[g] St. Mark xv. 46.
[h] St. Mark vii. 34, & St. John xi. 35.
[i] St. Luke vii. 14.

When Nurses[a] gently tend us,
    When Friends hold out their hands,[b]
When kind Physicians[c] cheer us,
    Or Priest with Chalice[d] stands:

In each we may discover
    The likeness of our Lord,
Who soothes our bed of sickness
    According to His word.[e]

O then, in joy or sorrow,
    Whatever may befall,
Let us our Lord remember,
    And see His Love in all.

---

[a] St. Mark i. 31.
[b] St. Mark viii. 23.
[c] St. Matt. viii. 16, 17.
[d] St. Matt. xxvi. 27.
[e] Psalm xli. 3.

Twilight.

THE Day is dying fast away,
   Beneath the clouds of vapour gray,
And the bleak wind, and driving rain,
Rattle against the window-pane,
And uncouth shadows rise and fall,
Thrown by the fire-light on the wall,
While my thoughts wander to and fro,
Among the Twilights long ago.

That pleasant pause!— too dark for sight,
Too soon to have the candle-light:
The children safely laid in bed,
Soft quiet in the small homestead,
Only the kettle's fire-side song,
Or murmurs, from the outward throng,
As quietly I used to wait,
And watch the sparks fall from the grate.

The footsteps passed along the street,
Until those came I sprang to meet ·

Then the strong arm was round my waist,
And loving words my spirit braced;
As we talked over all the day,
My weariness soon fled away:—
O tears, keep back! you shall not swell:
'Twas God Who took him—all is well.

A little longer,—I shall feel
That arm once more around me steal,
And hold me in a long embrace,
Where sin and sorrow have no place:
There, God Who gave him to be mine
Shall fill us full of Life Divine,
And of His pleasures, from their river,
Our souls shall drink, and drink for ever!

A little longer, trembling heart!
Let earth, and earthly joys depart;
A few more days, revolving slow,
Let a few Twilights come, and go,
Till life's appointed course is run,
And Grace its mighty work has done;
Then, O my Saviour, let me be
At home in Heaven, at home with Thee.

On the Death of a Child.

WITH tears we might not steep
    Thy calm and placid brow,
Thy gleaming golden hair
Shading a cheek too fair,
    Like sunbeams upon snow.

Beautiful ransomed clay!
    That calm was not of sleep:
It was the deep repose
Of a young life's last close;
    We knew, yet might not weep,—

But knelt beside thy couch,
    In silent agony;
All sin and pain were fled,
Death's Angel o'er thee shed
    A spotless purity.

All strewn with lilies pale,
  And robed in purest white,
In the still chamber thou,
With prayer and secret vow,
  Wast laid that mournful night.

Thy life's short sorrows past,
  Bright one, thou art at rest;
From our deep aching love,
Called to thy Home above,
  Thy Saviour's holy breast;

He Whose dear Name had power
  To cheer thy soul in death,
Lighting thy radiant eye,
Winning a soft reply
  From thy last trembling breath.

Therefore we may not weep,
  Because our prayers are heard:
From sin's deep bitterness
And the world's wilderness,
  Flown is our dove-like Bird.

To * *

OH! what a gift of melody there lies
    In that dear voice, whose low lamenting tone,
Amid the other voices that arise,
    Wins all my heart to hear its song alone,
Pouring its music through the general strain,
Like a fresh stream unmingled with the main.

E'en thus it rolled its tender tumult on,
    The GLORIA PATRI's solemn gladness through,
Sweet as the last notes of a dying swan,
    Mournful as unrequited love, and true,
Till, as the AMEN fell upon my ear,
It steadied into music strong and clear.

What deep emotions to my heart were brought,
    By the submissive cadence of that word!
The holy service fixed no more my thought,
    And e'en that Pastoral voice spoke on unheard,

As thy life's vanished years came thronging fast,
And, in processioned train, before me passed.

God's glory, through long ages, in a flood
   Its boundless splendours in vast billows rolled;
Yet thee, a thing of yesterday, His blood
   Bought at a costliness of price untold,
That thou, frail creature, by His grace should'st be
A crown and trophy of His victory.

He polishes the jewel year by year,
   With ceaseless care, and chisel sharp and keen,
Shedding Paternal drops of pity clear,
   Where the hot edges of the blade have been,
That thou may'st shine a fair transcendent gem,
For ever, in Jehovah's diadem.

He wills, His glory should by thee be shown,
   Thy patient cheerfulness, thy quiet faith,
Thy heavy cross borne silently alone,
   In His dear steps Who loved thee to the death.
Ah! is it difficult to say, Amen,
   With sweet unhesitating voice again?

TO * * *

Is not each deed of love, each thankful thought,
    Each secret prayer and uncomplaining sigh,
Each holy act in self-denial wrought,
    A GLORIA PATRI, that is heard on high
By Him Who quenched the light that on thee shone,
That thou might'st sun thee in His Love alone?

He is thy Father—and thy heart can tell
    The deep, deep meaning of that holy word;
A Father from Whose blessed lips "Farewell"
    Shall never through Eternity be heard:
By Him were all thy fine affections given;
Return them now, all sanctified, to Heaven.

Oh! in unshaken trust on Him depend;
    Let Hope's sure anchor through the veil be cast:
Soon shall these bitter struggles have an end,
    This weary-heartedness shall soon be past;
And thou and thy lost treasure shall above
Dwell in the calmness of untroubled love.

His Presence.

*" I the Lord thy God will hold thy right hand, saying unto thee,
Fear not, I will help thee."*

FEAR not, for I am here,
    To hold thy trembling hand,
To lead thee through the coming year,
    On to the better land.

Yes! I am with thee now,
    To watch that ransomed heart,
To see how in its woe
    It will perform its part.

Do not I know the thoughts
    That crowd across thy brain,
Whose sinking soul was once
    Susceptible to pain?

My unforgotten child,
   Have I not prayed and wept,
And through the silent night
   A lonely vigil kept?

Implicitly resign
   Into My care thy soul;
These hands, that wounded thee,
   Can they not make thee whole?

On other hopes than Me
   Thou hast leaned long, and hard,
They broke, and pierced thy spirit;
   They were not thy reward.

Then rouse thee, fearful one,
   And turn those downcast eyes
To where prophetic flashes
   In the far East arise.

So shalt thou calmly venture
   On through the wilderness,
Safe in My guiding power,
   My matchless tenderness.

O Sealed for Life Eternal,
  What mark is on thy brow?
The Cross of Him who suffered,
  For thee, and with thee now.

Fear not, thy Captain whispers
  The conflict may be hard,
But I am thy Deliverer,
  Thy Shield and thy Reward.

The Past.

O SPEAK not to her of the Past;—that word
   Is fraught with sense of pain;
'Tis like a song of home, in exile heard,
   An old familiar strain,
That makes us pause in sadness,
   And silently depart
To listen to its melody,
   With undivided heart.

O speak not to her of the Past, nor bear
   The weary wandering dove,
In the cold winter's melancholy air,
   Back to its nest of love;
The autumn winds have rent it,
   The songsters all are flown,
'Mid dying leaves and ice-drops
   It perisheth alone.

THE PAST.

It may be, carelessly thou speak'st some name,
    In an untroubled tone,
That once unto her ear like music came,
    In days for ever gone:
But now it is a talisman
    To waken thoughts of gloom,
Its well-known letters are inscribed
    On some far-distant tomb.

Or gaily thou recallest to her mind
    Some well-remembered scene,
Where sorrow that has left its sting behind,
    Upon her soul has been;
Or hopes that rose triumphantly
    Like arrows to the sky,
Like them too, sank back rapidly,
    And found no rest on high.

Then, Sister, speak not of the Past to one,
    Whose memory is so true
To thoughts and pictured scenes now changed and gone,
    And friends her childhood knew;
Her heartstrings are too finely strung,
    E'en for thy hands to touch;
They break, or grow discordant,
    At but one stroke too much.

Speak rather of the Future : bid her gaze,
   With Faith's untiring eyes,
Upon the distant rose and amber rays
   Now stealing o'er the skies :
Behind them lies a country,
   Upon whose golden strand
Time's waters lose their power,
   And trouble not the land.

O bid her listen to those words, 'The Past,'
   As they are spoken there,
As bells that toll awhile, then break at last
   In gladness on the air ;
Yes, music far more thrilling
   Than she hath heard of yore,
In undulating echoes
   Is wafted from that shore.

Tell her, the shipwrecked joys of other years
   Are landed on that coast ;
The deathless love, which she hath dimmed with tears,
   Hath there its sadness lost :
Ineffable tranquillity
   Over that Home is cast,
And only sin, and sorrow,
   Are left unto the Past.

H. L. P.

Easter, 1868.

THOSE little feet, that could not walk,
    Have climbed the golden stair;
Those silent lips, that could not speak,
    Break out in praise and prayer.

The hands that had such feeble hold
    Now grasp a golden Palm;
The heart that throbbed with suffering
    Is bathed in endless calm.

That weary head that could not rest
    Is crowned with garlands bright;
Those eyes, of mystery so full,
    Shine with unclouded light.

Therefore our Easter morn is glad,
    Because to us was given
A Holy Innocent, to yield
    Unto the Lord of Heaven.

I.

Satisfied.

March 20th, 1870.

RING high, ring clear,
   Ye bells of Heaven!
An entrance bright
   To him be given!

Open your ranks,
   Ye Angel bands,
To where the high
   Green Rainbow stands.[a]

Let him pass on,
   Unto the feet
Of Him he loved,
   And longed to meet.

Him he adored,
   And yearned to see,
With Whom his soul
   At rest will be.

[a] Rev. iv. 3.

Ring high, ring clear,
  Ye bells of Heaven!
The Morning Star
  To him is given.

II.

Asleep.

March 28, 1870.

TOSS, ye wild waves,
  Upon the shore;
He is at rest,
  For evermore.

Moan o'er the surf,
  Thou wind so drear;
Moan, sob, and wail;
  He will not hear.

Close by he lies;
  But a long sleep
His wondrous smile
  Enchained doth keep.

Roll, thou wild sea,
    Against the shore;
He is at rest,
    For evermore.

III.

Silence.

FROM infancy I had the right
    To win his glances tender,
And to his teaching, deep and wise,
    My spirit to surrender.

Now he is gone, and all is still;
    Tears make no noise is falling,
Nor sighs, too heavy to be heard,
    Nor names the heart is calling.

I sit alone, and all is still;
    Christ makes no sound in healing,
And silently the Comforter
    Works at the soul's annealing.

Here and There.

To I. K. *Christmas*, 1872.

How is it here? A quiet grave;
   A silence in the Hall;
A vacant place that none can fill;
   A shadow upon all.

How is it *There*? A wreath of light;
   A name that none can tell;
A palm-branch gathered by the Fount
   Where living waters swell!

Then friends, still hang your holly boughs,
   Still twine the Christmas Rose,
For she is nearer to you now
   Than when her voice arose

In Christmas Carols soft and clear,
   Whose echoes haunt you still
With sweetness that is set to grief,
   And longings nought can fill.

The bright home circle of All Saints
  Is filling in, right fast;
The children from their exile come,
  Earth's banishments all past.

Let melody of thankful joy
  Unto our God be given;
A little while—we too shall know
  What Christmas is in Heaven.

Sunset and Sunrise

July 19, 1873.

I.

ASLEEP he seemeth
  On his grassy bed,
Thyme and blue harebells
  Round his head;
While fern-leaves rustling
  In the sunshine fair,
Wave their green plumes around him,
  With triumphant air.

The tender shadows
  Falling from the hill,
Rest on the greensward
  Where he lieth still.
O wind, blow softly
  From the setting sun!
The noblest heart in England
  Its great work has done.

II.

Was it sunset only?
    Was it not sun-rise,
Where the radiant spirit
    Woke with "glad surprise?"

Everlasting Morning
    By the glassy sea,
Sea of fire and crystal
    Where the victors be.

He who fought with error,
    Firm and unenticed,
Suddenly translated
    To the smile of Christ.

He who bore God's Ark up
    With such steadfast hand,
Passed the River dryshod
    To the Heavenly land.

Still the silver trumpet
    Echoes from above,—
His, whose life was Duty,
    And his watchword "Love."

Let us mourn him nobly,
    Though with falling tears;
With no weak surrender,
    With no faithless fears.

Moses and Elijah
    Pass away from sight,
But the Lord remaineth,
    Leader of the fight.

Saviour, guard and guide us
    Through the darkening years,
Till the last have triumphed,
    Till the morn appears;

Everlasting Morning
    By the Crystal Sea,
Where the crowned and ransomed
    Shall abide with Thee.

Crowned.

June 17, 1874.

HER course fulfilled, she " fell asleep,"
Hushed into slumber, sweet and deep.
O Rest, well earned
By her, who turned
To make her home beneath the Cross,
Counting self-chosen ease as loss!

Fair story of a steadfast life,
Led in the shade, apart from strife:
Heart, calm and pure,
That would endure
God's perfect Will unto the end,
Knowing the Glory, to which sorrows tend!

Where is she now? Not where the breeze
Murmurs among the sheltering trees,
And shadows pass
Over the grass,
And sea-scents, brought from distant waves,
Are floating o'er the quiet graves.

She is on high;—her eyes have seen
The King Who had her Saviour been.
      O life fulfilled—
      In rapture stilled—
With Him Who led her, by the road
Of suffering, to be crowned of God!

A Fragment.

SAID I, a ceaseless stream of life passed on
    From Earth to Heaven? Yet there will come a
    pause.
There is a soul that shall one day go hence,
Of whom convoying angels will proclaim,
"This is the *last* that has to pass through Death."
Then, what a whisper, what a thrill will run
Through all the realms of Paradise, and sweep
On through the Courts of Heaven, and every star
Of Christ's great Universe! "He will go down,
His feet upon Mount Olivet shall stand:
Now is the Resurrection." . . . .

Missionary Hymn.

TELL it out among the people
    That the Saviour is the King;
With unceasing Alleluias
    Let the new creation ring.
Let a tide of intercession
    For the Spirit's quickening breath
Overflow the barren regions
    Still in darkness and in death.

Tell it out among the people
    That the Father sent the Son
To bring back to Him repentant
    A lost race by sin undone,
To illuminate their darkness
    With the Day-spring from above,
And to teach man's inmost spirit
    That the Father's Name is Love.

Tell it out among the people
    That the Saviour seeks the lost,
And has paid down as their Ransom
    His own Life's most mighty cost.

He, with ceaseless supplications,
  Intercedes for us above,
And has bid His Church bear record
  That the Saviour's Name is Love.

Tell it out among the people
  That the Spirit has come down,
And He still abides among us,
  The Redeemer's work to crown.
He renews us, heals us, helps us,
  Although weak and slow we prove,
And each contrite heart can witness
  That the Spirit's Name is Love.

Tell it out to every creature
  That the Lord will soon return
To rebuild the earth's waste places,
  And to comfort all that mourn :
That disease, and death, and danger
  From before Him will depart;
And, God's Love, at last victorious,
  He will reign in every heart.

"Our Light Affliction."

LORD! dost Thou call this our affliction "light?"
  Is all this anguish little in Thy sight?

"Child, bring thy balance out. Put in one scale
All thine afflictions; give them in full tale;
All thy bereavements, grievances, and fears;
Then add the utmost limit of man's years:
Now put My Cross into the other side,
That which I suffered, when I lived and died."

I cannot, Lord; it is beyond my might:
And lo! my sorrows are gone out of sight!

"Then try another way. Put in the scale
The glory now unseen, behind the Veil;
The glory given to be thine own estate;
Use that 'exceeding and eternal weight:'
Which kicks the beam?"

    Ah! Lord, Thy word is right;
Thus weighed, my sorrow doth indeed seem "light."

Welcomed.

November 16, 1874.

FOLLOW, follow, follow,
    Follow the glad flight
Of the soaring spirit
    To the Home of Light:
Veil thy face adoring,
    As she hears the word
That will bid her welcome,
    When she sees the Lord;—

Sees Him in His glory
    Human and Divine,
Where the twofold splendours
    On His brows combine:
For such height of blessing
    Unto man is given,
Christ to us is nearer
    Than aught else in Heaven!

Veil thy face adoring;
    Mortal cannot know

Of that wondrous meeting,
  The heart's overflow;
Its full transformation
  In that utter light;
The soul's consummation
  In its Saviour's sight.

When searched through with glory,
  And instinct with light,
With Love's burning lustre
  And Joy's deep delight,
He will give her entrance
  To the long, long line
Of the perfect spirits
  Who around Him shine.

O what bursts of greeting!
  O what outstretched hands,
And what jubilations
  Mid those saintly bands!
As the friends receive her,
  Whom she loved the most,
With the choral welcomes
  Of the angel host.

Fix thy gaze upon them,
  For the Grave is deep,
And thy heart is lonely,
  And thine eyes must weep;
And the shadows gather
  In the Home she left;
And while she rejoices,
  Thou art sore bereft.

Yet let glad Hosannas
  From thy heart arise;
For, though Earth is darkened,
  Thou hast still the skies;
And thy place is ready
  High above all sorrow;
Trust thyself to Jesus,
  And thou too shalt follow.

Alice.

Capetown, April 5, 1875.

FROM the unceasing swell
    Of the blue restless waves,
Inland they bore the lily form
    Unto those Southern graves.

The sunny Earth's warm breast
    Received her peaceful smile,
From life's short voyage laid to rest
    Just for a little while.

O Mother, Death is strong,
    But Christ is stronger still;
And the Death Angel in his wrath
    Does but fulfil His will,

Who from Earth's fairest things
    Takes some unstained away,
To be brought up beside His Throne,
    And dwell with Him alway.

And when the mighty hosts
 Of the redeemed shall meet,
All times, all races, circling round,
 Adoring at His feet,

Will not a special grace
 Of heavenly beauty rest
On those bright souls who, ere they sinned,
 Were taken to be blest,

Filled from the first with light,
 Filled with the Spirit's power;
Of our redeemed humanity
 The undefilèd flower?

O sight for eyes now dimmed
 With hot tears falling fast!
O morn of unimagined joy
 That evermore shall last!

"Even so, Lord Jesus."

YET one more whisper of Thy Name,
    A whisper low and deep,
A something that the heart would fain
    As its own secret keep;

But yet must tell, from pure amaze
    At Thy long-suffering grace,
That overflows our deepest needs,
    And sweeps away all trace

Of bitterness from out our griefs
    That unbelief has made.
Can grief be *bitter*, when we know
    It is but joy delayed :—

Joy set apart, that it may grow
    Unto a height of bliss
And beauty, in that other world,
    It could not reach in this?

And while it grows, above all fear
    Of danger or of sin,
The Lord by grief expands our hearts
    To take new blessing in.

Lord, fill our chasms with Thyself,
    For Thou all loss hast measured;
Yea, fill us fuller of Thyself,
    In Thee all gain is treasured.

But we are weak, and toss about
    For something that shall ease us;
Then come, and win from out our hearts
    An "Even so, Lord Jesus!"

THE END.

LONDON:
Printed by JOHN STRANGEWAYS, Castle St. Leicester Sq.

For the Sick and Sorrowful.

THE SHELTERING VINE.
Selections by the late COUNTESS OF NORTHESK.
With an Introduction by the Most Rev. R. C. TRENCH, D.D. Archbishop of Dublin. 9th Thousand. 2 vols. small 8vo. 10s. 6d.
Volume I. 6s.; Volume II. (on the Loss of Friends), 4s. 6d.

The object of this Work is to afford consolation under the various trials of mind and body to which all are exposed, by a Selection of Texts and Passages from Holy Scripture, and Extracts from Old and Modern Authors, in Prose and Poetry, with a Selection of Prayers adapted to the same.

SONGS IN THE NIGHT;
Or, HYMNS of HOPE and TRUST for WEARY WATCHERS.
Selected and Arranged by ANNA CLOWES.
Large cr. 8vo. in very large type, paper cover, 1s. 6d.; limp cloth, 2s.

'Selected with good judgment . . . Will no doubt prove a welcome companion to many of those who are afflicted or distressed.'—*Record.*

WORDS OF PEACE.
Or, THE BLESSINGS AND TRIALS OF SICKNESS.
By BISHOP OXENDEN, D.D.
58th Thousand. Fcap. 8vo. *large type*, cloth, 1s. 6d

THE HOME BEYOND; or, A Happy Old Age.
By BISHOP OXENDEN, D.D.
233rd Thousand. Fcap. 8vo. *large type*, cloth, 1s. 6d.
'*Words*' and '*Home*' together, roan, 5s.; morocco, 7s. 6d.

THE COVENANT OF LOVE.
A Manual of Devotion for the Sick and Suffering.
Being Twenty-eight Readings, with a Prayer and Hymn to each.
By A. M. JAMES, Author of 'Christian Counsels,' &c.
Square crown 8vo. cloth, 2s. 6d.; paper cover, 2s.

'Gentle, soothing, and at the same time ardently religious, t supplies just the special groove of thought which is needed for the sick-room.'—*Literary Churchman.*

STRENGTH MADE PERFECT
IN WEAKNESS. By A. M. JAMES
16mo. sewed, 2d.; or 1s. 6d. per packet of 12.

'A little tract, on tinted paper, in which is stated very simply and affectionately how Christian people may fail to find their Saviour's strength by not seeking more than His strength, that is Himself. The strength is to come, not from without, but as the branch derives its strength from the vine, by ultimate union with Christ.'—*Church Bells.*

For the Sick and Sorrowful.

LIGHT AT EVENTIDE.
Large-print Readings for the Sick and Aged.
Second Edition. Square crown 8vo. cloth, 1s. 6d.; in packet, 1s.

STRENGTH OF MY LIFE.
Large-print Readings for the Sick and Aged.
By the Author of ' Light at Eventide.'
Square crown 8vo. cloth, 1s. 6d. ; or in packet, 1s.

'Will be a great comfort and help to the class for whom it is designed'—*Christian World.*

WE WOULD SEE JESUS.
Large-print Readings for the Sick and Aged.
By Author of ' Light at Eventide,' ' Strength of my Life,' &c.
Square crown 8vo. cloth, 1s. 6d. ; in packet, 1s.

' Simple, but full of Gospel truths, especially adapted to direct and comfort those for whom they are written.'—*Our Own Fireside.*

THE SOUL'S COMFORT IN SORROW.
Being Selections from the Author's Poetical Writings.
By G. WASHINGTON MOON, F.R.S.L.
Demy 24mo. cloth, 2s. 6d. ; roan, 3s. 6d.

' In a time of trouble it would be found most suitable and salutary to the distressed and troubled.'—*Literary World.*

THE SOUL'S INQUIRIES ANSWERED.
A Daily Scripture Text-Book. Eleventh Edition.
By G. WASHINGTON MOON, F.R.S.L.
16mo. with blank leaves for Birthdays, &c. 2s. 6d. ; leather, 3s. 6d.
Cheaper Edition, cloth, 1s. 6d. ; leather, gilt edges, 2s. 6d.
Illustrated Edition, with 13 Photographs. Sm. cr. 8vo. cl. ex. 10s. 6d.

' A happy idea happily carried out. There is a question and an answer for every day of the year, while on the opposite page there is a blank diary intended for a treasury of the autographs of friends under their respective birthdays. The volume may be had with or without this last addition.'—*The Freeman.*

LONDON: HATCHARDS, PUBLISHERS, 187 PICCADILLY.

www.ingramcontent.com/pod-product-compliance
Lightning Source LLC
Chambersburg PA
CBHW020923230426
43666CB00008B/1546